Praise for *Why People Don't Believe You...*

"I have read many books on the topic of selling skills. Many are an entertaining way to spend an afternoon. Rob Jolles never fails to make you better! You will see results! You can't afford *not* to read this."
—**Ron Pratt, Head of North American Field Sales, Janus Henderson Investors**

"We seem to obsess about trying to find the right words to use. It's time to obsess about finding the right tune behind these words, and that's just what Rob Jolles has done. Bravo!"
—**Kathy Richman Wallace, VP Director of Sales Development, Ivy Distributors, Inc.**

"In a world awash in 'fake news' and 'alternative facts,' presenting yourself as a trustworthy source has never been more important, no matter what field you may be in. And the surprise in Rob's book is that *it's an inside job*. This is a must-read for anyone in a position of leadership."
—**Orvel Ray Wilson, CSP, CEC, coauthor of the legendary Guerrilla Marketing series**

"What always shines through is Rob's genuine passion for helping people succeed—whether they're sales professionals or the long-term unemployed. Now Rob has brought his wisdom and ideas together into an easy-to-read, immediately actionable book, *Why People Don't Believe You....* From learning how to believe in yourself to adopting the right tone and demeanor to back up your words, Rob has developed a playbook for sustainable, long-term success."
—**John Golden, Chief Strategy and Marketing Officer, Pipelinersales Inc.**

"Credibility is an elusive trait so many of us strive for, yet we find others may not see it in us. I've known and worked with Rob for over twenty-five years. No one understands the elements of credibility better than Rob Jolles. His perspectives on how we can improve the way we're perceived and our credibility are peerless."
—**Dana Klein, Vice President, Sales Strategy and Planning, American Beacon Advisors**

"Rob can take an everyday situation from his past and turn it into an extraordinary and valuable lesson in sales *and* life. His newest effort is the key to unlock a belief in your inner self to achieve unbounded success."
—**Douglas Heikkinen, Publisher, IRIS.xyz**

"Selling is both art and science, and successful professional selling is knowing how to blend just the right portions of both to create a customized story for each prospect. Rob Jolles has been teaching people how to do this for years, and now he's put this wisdom in a new book, *Why People Don't Believe You...*. Unless you have more business than you can handle, get your hands on Rob's new book. You'll thank me later."

—Jim Blasingame, award-winning author of *The 3rd Ingredient* and *The Age of the Customer*

"Part Zig Ziglar, part Dr. Phil, and part Jerry Lewis, Rob has impacted the 'tune' of those in career transition from unemployed to confidently employed! His practical yet powerful advice is easy to digest and can be implemented by anyone looking to develop more impactful relationships."

—Bob Korzeniewski, Executive Director, Career Network Ministry, McLean Bible Church

"I've watched Rob work his magic time and time again with folks who have taken the worst kind of blow to their confidence—the loss of their job. The tune they sing beyond his process is one we can all learn to carry in any role or situation. It's the undeniable tune of confidence."

—JV Venable, speaker, author, leadership coach, and Principal, Drafting, LLC

"Why read this book? Read it because every interaction you have with others matters, and Rob's thoughts will give you the understanding of what it takes to ensure you make and leave your mark with believability."

—Brian Walsh, Senior Director, Force Management

"Rob Jolles once again knocks it out of the park with this book. *Why People Don't Believe You...* takes a much closer look at the how-tos of communicating and really has opened my mind and my heart to improving this skill set. Read this book, apply the strategies, and enjoy the results—period!"

—Doug Sandler, bestselling author of *Nice Guys Finish First*

"Sight and sound function differently in the mind. Win the ears of the people, and their eyes will follow. Rob Jolles uses the energy of words and the sounds of words to show us the steps to being both believable and memorable."

—Robert E. Silvani, Executive Director, Mercury Capital Advisors

Why People Don't Believe You

Why People Don't Believe You

Building Credibility
from the Inside Out

Rob Jolles

BK

Berrett–Koehler Publishers, Inc.
a BK Business book

Berrett-Koehler Publishers, Inc.
1333 Broadway, Suite 1000, Oakland, CA 94612-1921
Tel: (510) 817-2277   Fax: (510) 817-2278   www.bkconnection.com

Ordering Information

Quantity sales. Special discounts are available on quantity purchases by corporations, associations, and others. For details, contact the "Special Sales Department" at the Berrett-Koehler address above.

Individual sales. Berrett-Koehler publications are available through most bookstores. They can also be ordered directly from Berrett-Koehler: Tel: (800) 929-2929; Fax: (802) 864-7626; www.bkconnection.com.

Orders for college textbook/course adoption use. Please contact Berrett-Koehler: Tel: (800) 929-2929; Fax: (802) 864-7626.

Distributed to the U.S. trade and internationally by Penguin Random House Publisher Services.

Berrett-Koehler and the BK logo are registered trademarks of Berrett-Koehler Publishers, Inc.

Printed in the United States of America

Berrett-Koehler books are printed on long-lasting acid-free paper. When it is available, we choose paper that has been manufactured by environmentally responsible processes. These may include using trees grown in sustainable forests, incorporating recycled paper, minimizing chlorine in bleaching, or recycling the energy produced at the paper mill.

Library of Congress Cataloging-in-Publication Data
Names: Jolles, Robert L., 1957– author.
Title: Why people don't believe you— : building credibility from the inside out / Rob Jolles.
Other titles: Why people do not believe you
Description: First Edition. | Oakland : Berrett-Koehler Publishers, 2018.
Identifiers: LCCN 2018023352 | ISBN 9781523095896 (paperback)
Subjects: LCSH: Business communication. | BISAC: BUSINESS & ECONOMICS / Business Communication / General.
Classification: LCC HF5718 .J575 2018 | DDC 650.1/3—dc23
LC record available at https://lccn.loc.gov/2018023352

25 24 22 21 20 19 18   10 9 8 7 6 5 4 3 2 1

Cover design by Ian Koviak, The Book Designers. Interior design and composition by Gary Palmatier, Ideas to Images. Elizabeth von Radics, copyeditor; Mike Mollett, proofreader; Rachel Rice, indexer.

*This book is dedicated to every person who
at some point in life lost his or her way and was misled
into believing they just weren't good enough.*

*I'm quite sure you are,
and if you believe it,
others will, too.*

CONTENTS

Foreword   ix

Preface   xiii

INTRODUCTION

It's Not the Words; It's the Tune   1

CHAPTER 1

Believing in Yourself   7

CHAPTER 2

Fear and Response   27

CHAPTER 3

Getting Others to Believe You   47

C H A P T E R 4

Stepping Up Your Game   69

C H A P T E R 5

Putting a Lion in Your Heart   89

C H A P T E R 6

Positivity!   109

C H A P T E R 7

The Politics of Success   131

C O N C L U S I O N

Moving beyond Hope   161

Suggested Readings   165

Acknowledgments   168

Index   170

About the Author   180

About Jolles Associates, Inc.   182

FOREWORD

Over the past 40 years, I have taught and lectured on success and achievement to more than 5 million people in 83 countries. I have always searched for the answer to the key question: *Why are some people more successful than others?*

Now, Rob Jolles, a talented and skilled author, teacher, and success coach, has identified one of the most important reasons for success and failure, happiness and unhappiness, ever discovered.

Based on his many years of working with thousands of people, he shows you exactly what you need to do to become the master of your life, to achieve your goals, and to break through any barriers (mostly mental) that might be holding you back.

Rob has invested hundreds of hours in study and teaching to conclude that your believability, credibility, and authenticity are the most important qualities you can develop to get people to trust you from the first moment of meeting.

He teaches that there is a direct relationship between how much you trust and believe in yourself and how much others trust and believe in you.

You learn a series of practical, proven techniques and actions that you can practice to be more believable and influential with each person you meet. You learn how to get and keep the job you really want and how to be seen as a leader in your work and personal life.

When I was growing up, coming from a poor and dysfunctional family, I never had any friends, at least not for very long. I spent most of my childhood alone or in the company of other unpopular kids. It never occurred to me that all personality skills are learnable, that by treating people in a certain way, they will trust and believe you from the first eye contact.

Interviews with personnel executives—those who do the hiring for large and small companies—found that their decision whether to hire someone was made largely in the first 30 seconds—from the first greeting, handshake, and response.

Sometimes I ask my audiences, "How much of decision-making is logical and how much is emotional?" They usually guess that the ratio is 80-to-20 or 90-to-10. I then explain to them that in truth it is 100 percent emotional. We decide emotionally and then we justify logically. Rob shows you how to immediately connect with people at a deep level emotionally and then move to logic and reason.

As a professional speaker, I must connect with my audience—often hundreds or thousands people—within the first 30 seconds and then maintain that connection for several hours, right up to the conclusion of the event. You can do the same with the people you meet.

The good news is that all relationship and personality skills are learnable with practice and repetition. You can learn any skill you need to improve the quality of your life. There are no limits.

Congratulations to you for reading this book. It can change your life forever.

Brian Tracy
Motivational public speaker
and self-development author

PREFACE

onducting seminars for over 30 years, logging more than 2.5 million miles in the air, and traveling around the world, I thought I understood what every audience needed. After all, when it comes to persuasion, I'd like to modestly put forward the notion that I am considered an expert. I have written books on the subject, I've consulted with countless Fortune 500 companies on the subject, and I've stepped in front of tens of thousands of people to tell them what I know about the subject. But back in the summer of 2012, nothing could prepare me for the audience I met in a church in McLean, Virginia.

I had received a call from my friend Will, who told me about a group that he had been volunteering to help for the past few years, and they needed good motivational speakers. He went on to tell me that the group was called Career Network Ministry (CNM), a nondenominational support group dedicated to helping those in career transition. I wasn't keen on the idea of speaking for free, but Will was persistent, and as the location was only about

25 minutes from my house, I figured I'd get in there, give them a show, and get home.

I heard my father's words loud and clear in my head, telling me, *You don't just give with your checkbook; you give with your time.* He walked that walk, dedicating more than 60 years of his life to the Boy Scouts of America and the Lions Club. Yep, I could give this group an hour or so of my time.

The presentation I planned to deliver was one I had given countless times. I figured teaching this group how to *sell*—with the product being themselves—would be just what the doctor ordered. Besides, it's not as though I don't take the talks I deliver seriously; but just how difficult could it be to teach a dozen or so folks how to sell themselves in a job interview?

The first thing I noticed when I walked into the Career Network Ministry was that the audience was larger than I had anticipated. There may have been 30 or so people milling around, lost in a rather large room. I was a little miffed because the room was way too big for this audience. I wanted a warmer environment, but as my intention was to put on a quick 60-minute show and get out of there, I wasn't going to make waves.

As I tinkered with my audiovisual equipment, I noticed that the group was slowly growing. There were now 60 people in the room. When I asked if the entire audience was present, I was told with a smile, "Oh, no;

most are in training. Some are in résumé development, some are in LinkedIn training, some are learning elevator pitches, some are going through orientation—and those are just the rooms I can think of right now."

About 30 minutes before I was to speak, the side rooms began to let out, and the audience swelled to about 200. I was floored. There were announcements about networking meetings, recruiters were going over specific job openings, and more. But what really floored me was something called a "victory lap." This part of the meeting was dedicated to allowing those who had found jobs to come up, tell their story, and inspire the group. Well, it worked all right—on *me*! I was so moved by the stories I heard that I delivered my presentation and instantly signed up to volunteer.

For the first few months, I worked hard at taking the sales skills I had taught and written about for so long and converting them for an audience who needed to sell themselves to an employer. I told them the types of responses to questions they needed to master, along with the kinds of questions to ask, and I proceeded to fail miserably. No one seemed to benefit from a word I was saying.

Assuming that these people just weren't using the right words, I began to *write* the answers for them. I wrote out the exact responses to questions they needed to master and the exact questions they needed to ask—and I failed

again. What I felt were sharp and believable words
sounded anything but when those I was working with
used them.

It was like listening to someone try to sing a song, and
all the notes were flat. Even worse, I began to realize
that those I was working with seemed to not be able to
hear the notes at all. In music, when someone cannot
reproduce a musical sound, we refer to it as being tone
deaf. I was trying to teach the "tune" of the words they
were saying, and I realized that, in a sense, they were
"tune deaf."

I began a journey focused on trying to help these
wonderful people who were being betrayed by the sounds
they were *not* making. Could someone who does not
naturally use things like pitch, pace, and pause to create a
believable tune be taught a *more* believable tune?

Once I realized that it wasn't the words that were failing
these people but rather the way they were *saying* them,
I began to formulate a workshop that focused on three
things that had nothing to do with words: acting, improv,
and overall confidence. To test my hypothesis, I set a
requirement for who would be eligible to attend the
program: the entire class was to be composed of individuals who were unemployed for a minimum of two years.
It turned out that half the class had been unemployed for
closer to five years.

I knew this would be a stretch for this audience and would require some time, so I wasn't looking to design a program that lasted a few hours—I wanted a few days. That would allow me to gain the group's trust and enable them to trust one another.

I limited the group to the first dozen people who signed up, and I carefully worked in a longer-than-usual icebreaker, and the group began to bond. It worked! Within a few hours, the participants trusted the environment they were in and began to self-disclose at a deep level.

We started with simple vocal exercises that allowed me to demonstrate my own balanced feedback and my careful control of the group's balanced feedback, as well. No one would be harmed by unintentional but insensitive feedback on *my* watch! It worked. Participants began to open up, experiment, and explore while working through a series of tactics, small-group exercises, and individual presentations—all designed to teach—and then auditioning a tune they had never sung before.

Unencumbered by memorized or scripted words that had held them back and instead focusing on *how* they were speaking, we discovered what had been lacking for far too long: confidence. The words they had been seeking—their authentic words—became easier to find with their new self-assuredness, and they grew comfortable saying them.

The workshop ended, and what happened next was incredible: 10 of the 12 attendees were hired within two months! I walked around looking like the cat that had swallowed the canary, quite full of myself. I carefully went over my notes and made some minor adjustments, and I couldn't wait to try the workshop again.

A few weeks later, with a ridiculously large grin on my face, I sauntered up to my friend Bob, the true leader of CNM, and smugly said, "Have you heard about the numbers?! Ten out of 12, Bob, 10 out of 12! It worked!"

He looked at me with a knowing smile and said, "Helping them to be believable and getting them hired is one thing. Can you *keep* them hired?"

Keep them hired? I'd thought my work was done, and I hadn't spent one second thinking about whether what we had accomplished could be sustained. Sure enough, within a few weeks one of my "tune-mates," as I affection-ately called the workshop participants, came back. Then another came back, and then another. Within six months 40 percent of those who'd been hired were once again unemployed.

I had stumbled on a process that helped people who lacked the ability to get others to believe them, but, unfortunately, I had missed the part about sustainability. With a little less bounce in my step, I went back to the drawing board with an eye toward adding to the agenda some basic people politics.

All of us are visited by bad luck now and then, but, studying this rotating audience of close to 200 people a night, which was in a sense a human petri dish, I noticed an inordinate amount of "bad luck" when it came to getting along with colleagues and managers at work. The same sort of inability to hear the sounds they made was also playing out in their inability to see how others interpreted their actions.

Some of the most basic workplace skills—like knowing how to get along with your boss, or work with a team, or admit you are wrong—were consistently lacking. Even more troubling was that most of them had no idea they lacked those skills. That's why, at the end, this book turns to sustaining the belief that others have in you.

As soon as people skills were added to the workshops I was teaching, we saw participants not only get employed but stay employed.

Problem solved: But what about the rest of the population?

As I began telling my clients about how the workshops trained people in a more innovative way, I started hearing from other groups who were struggling to be believed. It was interesting to hear their stories because most had conceded that this would always be an issue, so they compensated. They found jobs that didn't require a connection with people or a need to be believed.

These are the people who will tell you, "I can't sell" and bristle at even the word *sell*.

But life can turn on a dime, and it's rare that people can stay employed at work, or even function effectively with family and friends, without the need for others to believe them. When this happens, they face the same struggles with this issue as everyone else.

We don't talk much about those who struggle to be believed.

But when you look at the number of people who are affected by it in one way or another, it may just be one of the most significant personality epidemics our society faces.

There's a reason why people don't believe you. This book will help you learn not only the skills necessary to make yourself more credible but also the proper attitude to sustain it. Everyone could use a tune-up now and then, and I am more than willing to be your guide. Come on in and let's get started.

It's Not the Words; It's the Tune

WORDS.

Oh my, how we *love* our words. We learn to write them letter by letter, then form them sentence by sentence, then assemble them paragraph by paragraph, and continue page by page. At one moment we can make people laugh at them and at another make people cry at them. We have been raised to believe that words are one of the most essential tools an individual can use to communicate.

Well, I say we have been sold a bill of goods. We've been duped. If words are so important, why are so many of us literally afraid to send a text or an email because we are nervous that our words will be misinterpreted? Could it be because our words alone offer little in the way of help when it comes to conveying the true emotional content of what we are trying to say? I am not suggesting that words don't have their place, but I contend that their place is overrated—*way* overrated.

The fact is, a huge percentage of the population struggles with an issue that has very little to do with the words we use: the simple act of being believed. We can find ways to mask this problem, but it haunts us just the same. We take jobs that don't require face time with clients, but we can't avoid interacting with members of our team. We avoid social situations that make us uncomfortable, but certain get-togethers cannot be avoided.

Given time we become masters at shielding our lack of confidence. The better we become at hiding, the bigger the problem becomes, and the bigger the problem becomes, the more insulated we are from changing our behaviors. Eventually, we get backed into a corner. Although desperate to get others to believe us, we are out of practice and out of confidence, and we instinctively fall back on our words to save us. When those words fail and, given this all-too-common scenario, they almost always do, we retreat even deeper into doubt.

We can't get others to believe us because we don't believe ourselves.

It's not the *words* that betray us; it's the way the words are used. I call that the "tune." Listening to words is like watching a magician work their magic. There is a place the magician wants your attention to be, and they will go to great lengths to keep your attention on a prop—but that distraction is to keep you from looking at their *other* hand. Words are where your attention may be, but the tune is where the magic happens.

It seems so simple, really. If so many people are struggling not with the words they say but with how they say them, why not focus on "soft skill" techniques like those found in this book? As crazy as this may sound, I believe one reason is because of two words in the previous sentence. The time has come to blow the whistle on two words that do well on their own but must never be put side-by-side: *soft skills.*

What exactly are soft skills? The term refers to competencies such as communication, time management, problem solving, working with teams, selling, negotiating, and basically learning how to work well with others. A common definition of *soft skills* is being able "to interact effectively and harmoniously with other people." Sounds pretty good so far.

Sadly, the term *soft skills* has a public relations problem. For instance, what do you think of when you hear the word *soft*? Its many definitions include "demanding little work or effort." Is it any wonder why the first thing to be cut from a company's training budget is the training in soft skills? Who would want to fund programs that teach skills that demand little work or effort?

If you Google the word *hard*—*soft*'s evil twin—you'll see it defined as "requiring a great deal of endurance or effort." So, it sounds like hard skills are those that you can really sink your teeth into. Hard skills refer to such noble tasks such as typing, writing, math, reading, and the ability to use software programs.

Here's a simple question: When was the last time you heard of someone losing their job, losing a key client, or being derailed in their life because they couldn't type well enough, do math in their head accurately enough, or use software efficiently enough? These are rarely the issues that hold us back because if there is a deficiency in any of these areas, there are numerous options to enable you to correct it.

By contrast, soft skills are less tangible and harder to quantify, but they are so much more important. As a matter of fact, the more you study what soft skills are, the better you'll understand how crucial they are to success. That's why I believe it should insult any rational person's intelligence to see soft skills being dismissed when they are critical, sometimes life-altering talents that are clearly undervalued.

Most people who struggle to be believed aren't struggling because their hard skills failed them. They are struggling because no one ever taught them how to bond fast enough, how to align with the right people well enough, how to be quiet quickly enough, how to connect with clients effectively enough, or, dare I say, how to sell well enough. No one ever taught them the soft skills they needed to be successful because there aren't enough places that address them.

You don't find many programs in schools because who would want to even advertise a class in something called soft skills? So, let's change the name once and for all. I've kicked around a few terms like *people skills* and

survival skills, but for me the winner is *performance skills.*
Those two words add respect and urgency to this vital set
of workplace proficiencies.

The term *performance skills* does justice to one of the most
important sets of competencies you will ever acquire.
These skills will be pivotal in determining whether you are
hired, accepted by others, promoted, admired, respected,
and more.

This book is about finding the necessary magic to help
others believe you. It requires a belief *in* you, so we start
there. The book moves on to tactics that will help others
believe you. It then focuses on maintaining courage and
confidence in yourself when doubt naturally creeps in,
and it concludes with a discussion of sustaining your
newfound credibility.

1

Believing in Yourself

Three vital words: *believing in yourself.* If *you* don't believe in you, it's nearly impossible for others to do so. How many times have you heard phrases like *If you want it badly enough, you can do it!* If only it were that easy. As a matter of fact, magically getting something because you want it so badly not only is a cliché but it clearly holds you back.

You hear it in sports all the time, particularly after a team has won a big game: "We just wanted it more than they did!" The thought of wanting something more than others seems to answer many questions, but to me it seems trite and misleading. If only succeeding in life were as easy as just wanting things more than those around you do.

Don't get me wrong: wanting something badly is not a completely useless attitude; it's just overrated. I have coached soccer and basketball teams for more than 25 years, and I could never attribute a team victory to just wanting it more. As a matter of fact, I am quite sure that if I ever wandered into the losing team's locker room, I would not hear that they just didn't want to win as badly as we did. When we were well prepared, practiced hard, and had an intelligent game plan, we were usually successful—but we did not pin our aspirations on just wanting it more. That would have provided a false sense of hope and been a waste of energy.

One of the most defining qualities we can possess is the simple capacity for self-confidence. It sure sounds simple, but for those who grapple with this humble notion, it can be life altering. Those who struggle have no doubt heard these encouraging words from family, friends, and coworkers: "You just have to believe in yourself." If only it were that easy.

Believing in *you* cannot be accomplished simply by wanting it or by being told to do it. It requires preparation, practice, and execution involving a set of skills that, over time, can be mastered. Having mentored those who wrestle with this fundamental life principle, I've discovered a clear set of skills that are natural for some and require practice by others—but they are obtainable by all!

I find it helps to break the process of believing in oneself into five steps, but you can sum them up in one big shift: you'll get there when you are willing to take the actions that others have taken to believe in *themselves*.

Commit to Believing

It always amazes me how determined those who struggle to believe in themselves can be. If *not* believing increased our chances of success by even 1 percent, I'd make it a competition and I would put it in every curriculum I deliver, but that is not the case. Not only is it logical to believe in oneself but it's completely within our power. Even the most hesitant human being can probably remember a time in childhood when it was easy to believe they'd grow up to be a firefighter, an astronaut, or anything else they aspired to be.

When you believe in yourself, it becomes a whole lot easier to get others to believe in you, as well. That means trusting yourself with the decisions you make—and that involves risk. But you can't believe halfheartedly; you must *commit* to believing in yourself all the way. That means deciding to believe and staying committed to that belief. Oh, if you don't, you might fall into something I call the squirrel syndrome.

It turns out we can learn a lesson or two from a squirrel. When you stop and think about it, the squirrel is an amazing animal; nature thought about *almost* everything when putting this furry creature together. Squirrels are fast, strong, agile, and clever; but, like many other creatures, the squirrel does have one significant imperfection: an inability to decide. The results of this tragic flaw can be clearly seen on many of our roadways.

We have all probably seen this sad scenario play out: We are driving along and see a dot in the distance. It darts into the road with lightning speed and ample time to make it to the other side—and then something happens: The squirrel begins to question its decision. As the gap between your car and that squirrel closes, the squirrel decides that maybe this *isn't* the time to cross the road. It chooses to race back to the other side.

Behind the wheel, we mutter to ourselves, "Come on, little buddy, *commit.*" As if on cue, the squirrel does decide—to once again change its mind. The ample cushion of time has now shrunk, resulting in a dangerous dash for the other side. As our car bears down, the squirrel could still be successful if only it didn't again question the choice it had made. What makes matters worse, the animal is so lost in its indecision whether to go right or left that it stands lost in the middle of the road. Even when we hit our brakes, it is often sadly the last decision that poor squirrel ever makes.

But there's a lesson to be learned from the squirrel syndrome, and this lesson plays out in much of what we do. When it comes to believing in ourselves, we are faced with two distinct paths to take. All we need to do is decide—and yet we often get caught up in our inability to commit.

Surely, there are times when good, solid, responsible decision-making assures us that the risk before us is worth taking. Now is the time to step off the curb and make a committed decision to believe in yourself. A well-known quote by John A. Shedd that hangs in my office reads: "A ship in harbor is safe, but that is not what ships are built for."

That dot in the road is now you, and your desire to overcome your hesitancy pushes you forward. Your inner voice tells you to take a courageous leap of faith and bound across that road. As the time to commit and act looms, another voice tries to horn in, encouraging you to step back and reassess this potentially risky decision. Neither voice is necessarily right or wrong, but the cognitive dissonance can have devastating results. We lean toward the act that requires risk, yet we attempt to mitigate that risk by taking a somewhat safer position to protect us if we fail. In so doing, we wind up committing to nothing. We are in the weakest, most vulnerable position: stuck in the middle of the road with no place to hide.

Of course, you have various options to help you decide: You can read this book, or seek the advice of others, or conduct research, or look to benchmark, or assemble whatever data you may wish to collect. The problem is, you may find that you're right back where you started and you still need to decide. Your committing to a decision is as challenging and as critical as it is for the squirrel.

You know what decision *I* want you to make—I'm waiting for you on the other side of the road! When you make it across, regardless of what other struggles await you, own the decision you had the courage to make.

Once you commit to believing in yourself and summon the courage to trust that decision, you can shift the focus to your personal effort. You will find a lot more success by redefining it as "making the personal effort that *I* can

control." And in the words of John Shedd, it really *is* what
you are built for!

Allow Yourself to Try—and Fail

For those who do not know me personally, I am a highly
competitive human being, to put it mildly. I enjoy winning and have never been a fan of losing. It's the third
option, however, that really disappoints me: not trying at
all. If you think back to some of your greatest accomplishments, I would bet that they were not achieved without
the risk of failure. As a matter of fact, I am sure you'll
agree that the greater the achievement, the greater the
risk of failure. In a strange way, failure is a teammate of
success, as opposed to being its evil twin. I have never met
a person who hasn't experienced both, and yet failure—
or the fear of failure—often seems to be the louder and
stronger of the two.

*The fear of failure sneaks
into our subconscious and
undermines our desire to try.*

Once inside our minds, the fear of failure paints a series
of worse-case scenarios, and before we realize it we retreat
from whatever it was we were about to try.

But what if we redefined success as a willingness to fail? What if we celebrated both our wins *and* our losses by the effort we extend and the courage we display in our brave attempt to try? I would wager that we'd be celebrating a whole lot more victories! What's more, our success would clearly be under our control, which would then breed more confidence, which would underpin more faith in ourselves.

Once upon a time when we were young, we truly believed that if we tried as hard as we could, we would be victorious. We weren't afraid to try because success was defined by what we learned from our experience, whether we won or lost. We not only believed in ourselves but also improved each time we tried. Somewhere along the way, that was coached out of us. Consider this simple Japanese proverb: *Failure teaches success.*

I think we had it right when we were too young to even question it. Believing in yourself has everything to do with allowing yourself to try. You *must* encourage yourself to try. The worst that could happen is that you fail. But don't you agree that doing nothing due to the fear of failure is worse than failure itself? With that encouragement and your willingness to attempt something new, you will ultimately find one of the greatest successes you can ever achieve: a belief in yourself.

Try to See Yourself as Others See You

Most people are unable to see themselves as others see them, and a by-product of this blind spot is doubt. You usually cannot attribute doubt to one particular aspect but rather a handful of them. When these aspects are addressed one by one, that doubt monster shrinks back under the bed. Shifting the angle of your own personal observation, much like an artist, can help.

We can learn a lot from artists. For example, have you ever watched an artist examine their own work of art? Part of the evaluation of that artwork occurs just by looking hard at it or walking past it. You might be surprised to learn what my wife, an artist, considers her two favorite ways to evaluate her work.

One of her methods is to go to the biggest mirror in our house. She holds up her painting for a long time, and she scrunches up her face, as though she is seeing that work for the first time. In fact, from the perspective that the mirror provides, she *is* seeing it anew. The image is in reverse, so she views the composition in an entirely new way. It gives her objectivity and the ability to see her work with fresh eyes.

The second way is with her camera. She'll shoot a few digital pictures of the work and either print them out or look at them onscreen. You would think that a picture of a picture would not be of much value, but she swears that she can see aspects of her work that her natural perspective just doesn't perceive.

She is working through a problem that is a challenge for many artists: it's difficult to see their work as others see it. The mirror and the camera are two classic ways to address this. Those of us who are not artists must learn to manage a similar situation.

Most people are unable to see themselves as others see them.

This is not just a minor blind spot; it can be a significant roadblock on our path to success. Without an alternative perspective, like an artist has, it's nearly impossible to see things as others see them.

When Xerox had its instructors conduct two-week training programs, every day the trainees would be video-recorded role-playing sales calls. The script each student followed was detailed and measurable, and instructors meticulously critiqued every behavior.

The instructors were trained to make few or no comments about trainees' personal traits, such as appearance, gestures, and facial expressions, because each night the students' homework was to evaluate their own performance and provide written feedback in the morning.

Watching the videos gave them a different perspective on how they looked and acted. The objective feedback was every bit as powerful as comments from the professional trainers.

To this day I frequently use that tool when I am coaching individuals or small groups. I bring out my smartphone or iPad and record their role plays or presentations, and I make the videos immediately available to them. I want them to see themselves as others see them, which is usually vastly different from the way they see themselves.

Sometimes this takes a little creativity. Whether it's a mirror, a photograph, a video, or a friend, we cannot trust our personal instincts alone. When you can see yourself as others do, you can make great strides—including chipping away at self-doubt, which enables you to take another step forward to believing in yourself.

Balance Your Personal Feedback

It never ceases to amaze me just how tough we can be on ourselves. That toughness is front and center when it comes to self-evaluation. We just aren't that nice to ourselves. Maybe it's human nature to focus on negative feedback, but positive observations are critical as well. If someone is unaware of something positive that they fail to see in themselves, even though others see it, that strength can easily be lost.

Improving your ability to coach yourself is another
important step in removing doubt and believing in you.
Performed halfheartedly, the results can be minimal at
best; but when done properly, the results can be powerful.
Here I share a three-step exercise designed to not just
improve your own performance but to gain confidence
and evolve. When you have an opportunity to self-access
while standing in front of a mirror or watching a clip of
yourself, consider the following steps.

Step 1 Ask yourself to identify two areas in which
you felt you did well. It's natural to be overly critical
of our own performance, so get ready for a tussle with
yourself. But remember: if you do not focus on a couple
of positives, what guarantee do you have that you can
repeat those positives? Making yourself consciously aware
of your strengths puts those behaviors ahead of the need
to be aware of both the good and the bad. The positives
default to the forefront.

But there's another, more subtle reason why I always
recommend starting with the positives. By doing so you
are conditioning your mind to look for and focus on your
strengths. It will be challenging at first, but think of how
healthy it will be when the first observations you instinctively make about yourself are positive ones.

Step 2 Ask yourself to identify two areas in which you
feel you could improve. Net out these deficiencies and

dig deeper for ideas on how you intend to fix them. Sometimes a good way to get started is to ask yourself, *What would I do differently if I performed this task again?*

Remember: your goal is not to just *identify* areas that need improvement but to strategically *address* them. When you identify what needs improving, choose solutions that are actually obtainable. That might mean breaking the solution into smaller steps. You can't, for example, get a college degree overnight, but you *can* enroll in a night class to help you fill in some gaps in your training.

Step 3 Finish with an encouraging remark or a pat on the back. This allows you to feel motivated, positive, and upbeat.

What should you have accomplished when this exercise is over? First, by limiting yourself to two positives and two areas for improvement, there is just enough to feel good about and just enough to work on. Consider the adage *If you emphasize everything, you emphasize nothing.*

Typically, after two or three times, this self-evaluation exercise becomes second nature. You need only sit back and listen to yourself methodically lay out what you did well, what you need to improve, and how you intend to make that improvement.

The strength in balancing your personal feedback is that it ensures fairness in sensitive areas. Unfortunately, most of us aren't in the habit of being nice to ourselves, and you are not helping if you beat yourself up or make sweeping criticisms like *What do I need to improve? How about everything!*

Control the Negative Voices

A few years ago, *Time* magazine ran an article titled "What Our Internal Voices Say about Ourselves," and sadly these aren't always productive conversations. Once these voices turn negative, it can be a slippery slope— but not if we stop underestimating this inner dialogue.

We all hear the voices, and we usually hear them when we're alone. They wait until they sense a vulnerable opening, like a bacterium seeking to infect a wound, and they can affect our ability to believe in ourselves. The voices seep into our conscious mind from our subconscious; they can begin as whispers, and before you know it can turn into shouts.

These negative voices are insidious and they exaggerate. They tend to pick at our confidence and belief in ourselves, and many of us underestimate them. As a matter of fact, often they disguise themselves as humorous personal barbs. We've all heard them.

▶ When you stub your toe, they can sound something like this: *Really? Have you lost your ability to walk into a room without hurting yourself?*

One poke seems harmless enough, but the voices are *not* harmless—and they never stop at just one poke. They pick up steam and wait for the next opportunity.

▶ When you can't figure out an answer to a question, they can sound something like this: *Oh, come on now; even **you** can figure this out.*

▶ When you get lost: *Maybe you should tattoo the directions on your arm because you can't seem to remember **anything** anymore.*

The voices may seem teasing, but do you still think their words are harmless? Do you think they cannot undermine your self-worth? They are, after all, *your* words—and sometimes you might actually say them out loud.
I suppose if they chirped in your ear only now and then, they wouldn't be so damaging, but they come in waves.
If you listen to them, your mind can become an echo chamber, reinforcing the negative and drowning out the positive. Would you like them to stop? They won't. And the more you listen to them, the meaner they get.

▶ When you feel defeated, they can sound something like this: *You aren't **good enough** to win.*

▶ When you feel lonely: *You **deserve** to be alone.*

▶ When you feel insecure: *You aren't **smart enough** to succeed.*

I reject the premise that these voices are teasing, I don't find them funny, and I am asking you to agree with me. It's difficult to stifle the voices while they hide in your subconscious, but the moment they infect your conscious mind, you can choose to not listen—and you can certainly choose to not say them out loud. The voices may very well try to convince you that you can't resist them, but you sure as heck can.

In the movie *A Beautiful Mind* (2001) starring Russell Crowe, when Professor John Forbes Nash Jr. is asked about the things he sees and hears, he does not declare himself free of their torment. Instead he says, "I've gotten used to ignoring them and I think, as a result, they've kind of given up on me. I think that's what it's like with all our dreams and our nightmares...We've got to keep feeding them for them to stay alive."

There are other voices you can choose to listen to, and these are the ones I encourage you to feed. These are the voices that tell you that *anyone* can stub a toe, or struggle to answer a question, or get lost, or feel defeated, lonely, or insecure. It's part of the human condition, part of being alive. It's also part of being kinder to yourself that contributes to believing in yourself, and we can all benefit from kinder voices.

Don't Wait to Celebrate

When you take the five steps—commit to believing, allow yourself to try and fail, try to see yourself as others see you, balance your personal feedback, and control the negative voices—you will probably stumble once or twice. Let's face it: when we struggle to believe in ourselves, there seems so little to celebrate because victories can be few and far between. But there's nothing like a well-deserved celebration after a hard-earned win. One seems to feed off the other; and like peanut butter and jelly, victory and celebration just seem to be made for each other. Call me a contrarian, but I think when there seems little to celebrate, a celebration is even *more* important.

During times of struggle, acknowledging and celebrating small victories makes sense—and there is no downside. Think of the last time you celebrated *any* victory; were you stronger or weaker from the experience? And please don't tell yourself that there is nothing to celebrate be- cause that's just not true. That's the negative voices talking.

There are a lot of things you can celebrate and pat yourself on the back for—even amid great struggles. What about your resolution to keep trying? How about celebrating the amount of effort you've put into something? Why not acknowledge the courage you've displayed by putting yourself in uncomfortable situations in your quest to succeed? Why shouldn't you feel good about how you continue to learn from your mistakes? How about giving yourself kudos for following your plan and pursuing your goals—regardless of the results?

When we struggle, we aren't starving for food; we're starving for joy.

A few years ago, I was hired to coach a team of 10 sales-people for a year. One of my favorite members of that team was a woman who had a tremendous will to succeed, but it had been battered by the company's sales manager, who could only see her failing sales numbers and not her potential. She was treated poorly and, having spent the previous two years as the lowest-performing sales rep on the team, lost faith in her ability to succeed.

Interestingly enough, her first year with the company was very profitable. I wanted to find a victory of sorts for her, so one of the first things I did was design a contest that involved the sales process this team was learning, rather than the actual results of selling. I felt that this would allow her to focus on something that was completely under her control: her effort. It worked, and she stormed past her teammates and won the contest.

What happened next was even more remarkable. The victory spurred in her a different, more confident mind-set that began to pay big dividends in the way she approached her clients. She went on to lead her company in sales for the next four years.

Allowing yourself to seek out and celebrate victories, no matter how small, will nourish your mind and body at a time when you need that sustenance the most. That in turn will have a direct impact on your ability to be more competitive in your larger, all-important challenges to come. So, don't be afraid to give yourself a pat on the back. Here's to your impending celebration!

To get others to believe you, you must first believe in yourself. The mind is your most powerful ally, and I can assure you that for its own self-preservation, it *wants* you to believe. Don't overthink it, and don't let doubt get in the way. Are you ready to keep going? Then follow me.

2

Fear and Response

Taking action to improve self-esteem can stir up fears in anyone. Those fears can dramatically increase when pressure is involved. I can assure you that you are not alone and that there is a constructive response to every fear.

Eleanor Roosevelt was known for her very gracious and sincere public image, and she was tremendously sensitive to the underprivileged. She described herself growing up as awkward and uncomfortable around others. Abraham Lincoln was admired as a man who could charm anyone he crossed paths with, and yet it is well known that he was an introvert who struggled with everyday conversations.

What did these two great leaders have in common? Both understood the value of reaching out to others, both were fantastic at it, and neither possessed a natural skill to accomplish that feat—but they believed in themselves, and they overcame their fears. It's just a matter of identifying your fears and applying a response to them. So, let's strip away some fears and expose them for what they really are: myths, misunderstandings, and communication inhibitors.

Fear: **The Odds Are against Me**
Response: **Begin by Showing Up**

When was the last time you were faced with an uncomfortable and challenging situation and you seriously considered the many reasons why you didn't need to go through with it?

You are not unique if the voices in your head are telling you that the odds are against you—we all must battle those voices. The voices you hear are sneaky because rather than tell you to quit, they find a more enticing solution: they tell you to just not show up. Not too long ago, I faced a situation that put me at odds with these voices.

The short story goes like this: I signed up for a race, a 2-mile swim that I've competed in a handful of times over the years. In the previous years, I was well trained for the event, and the race was not that difficult. But this year was different: I *knew* the race was going to be hard. As the date approached, I had a queasy feeling. It was fear. I had a bunch of things to worry about:

▶ Unlike previous years, I was unable to train like I had expected to. I was nursing an injury that cut my training swims down by two-thirds.

▶ Unlike previous years, rather than increase my training as the date approached, I had minor surgery that kept me out of the water altogether for four of the last six weeks before the swim.

▶ Unlike previous years, I was unable to secure a wetsuit, and the water was running cold at 67 degrees.

▶ Unlike previous years, I knew my time would be
slower and my chances of winning or placing in my
age group were slim to none.

So, I did what most of us instinctively do: I tried to
convince myself to simply not show up. Why should I?
This was certainly not going to be fun, and I knew
I was probably going to get kicked and punched by
faster swimmers.

The more I thought about it, the idea of just not showing
up sounded more and more appealing. After all, if I didn't
race, I wouldn't have to deal with the disappointment
of losing. Considering all of my darned good excuses,
not showing up sounded like the responsible thing to
do! Armed with my boatload of excellent excuses, not
showing up took hold as a legitimate option. Unfortunately, another word for not showing up cut through the
excuses and nagged my conscious mind: *quitting*.

Perhaps you don't like the word *quitting*. Would *giving up*
be a better way to describe it? Doing things outside our
comfort zone always brings out the excuses. Maybe it's
calling a client who makes you nervous, or confronting
a difficult situation, or going to a meeting you'd rather
skip, or attending an event that may take too much effort.
I could go on. We all have moments in our lives that
make us uncomfortable. I have a two-word answer to
anyone who questions whether they should do something

outside their comfort zone: *show up*. Use it as a battle cry. Make it your mantra.

I really had no idea if I was going to compete in that swim, but I made a promise to myself: I would not take the cowardly way out and quit while sleeping in my warm bed. I packed my swim bag the night before, set my alarm for 6 a.m., and made a deal with myself: if I showed up, stood on the shoreline, and decided it was not my day to jump in, I'd allow myself to *not* swim that race.

The next morning I got up, showed up, and never considered *not* jumping into that water. For the record, my lack of training slowed my time down, the injury I was nursing made itself known throughout the race, I was cold, and I got kicked and punched plenty of times. But I didn't quit before the race, and once I was in the water, quitting was not an option.

I'd like to tell you that completing that swim carried extra meaning, but in fact it did not. In the real world, lack of preparation rarely rewards us with a meaningful victory. But it did remind me how fragile the line between fear and courage can be, as well as how enticing the idea of just not showing up can be. What's more, can you imagine how much easier it would be to just not show up the next time you felt fear or nervousness about something?

Finding a comfortable way to quit is no way to train the mind. When a fighter faces overwhelming odds and

knows he may take a beating, no *real* fighter quits on his
stool. It is true that when you show up, you may have
to face some of your worst fears. It may be that pushing
past your fears will put you in a humbling situation.
If that's the case, dust yourself off and learn from it. I can
assure you: however insecure you may feel, it will pale in
comparison to the disappointment in yourself that comes
from quitting. As Woody Allen asserted, "Eighty percent
of success is showing up."

The next time you feel those butterflies in your stomach
and your mind presents you with a comfortable way to
not show up, symbolically set your alarm clock, pack your
bag, and get yourself to the shoreline. If you do, I'd bet
that regardless of what's holding you back, you'll jump
right in.

Fear: **I Can't Be Perfect**
Response: **Take Pride in Imperfection**

Pushing ourselves to do our best is clearly one of the keys
to success, but don't confuse the noble act of trying our
best with the noble act of pushing ourselves to perfection. They may sound similar, but they are dramatically
different. Doing our best requires discipline to take no
shortcuts in our effort and perform at our very finest.
But perfection is a whole different story, and the pursuit
of it can do far more to destroy what we are attempting
than to perfect it.

We can control our effort, but we cannot control our outcome.

Remembering this helps us optimize both. It is not a crime to pursue perfection; it's just misguided. If even one shred of evidence existed to prove otherwise, I'd be a fan, but the pursuit of perfection only works against us. After all, one of the greatest strengths we possess—when we perform at our highest level—is the ability to perform unencumbered by tension. Do you believe for one second that focusing on perfection *decreases* tension?

Perfection is attained on rare occasions, but it is not something to which the best of the best actively aspire. Someone who does achieve perfection will likely tell you that they did not even contemplate perfection while apparently accomplishing it. They knew that the mere thought of it would cause tension that would inhibit their performance.

Late in a baseball game when a pitcher is in the position to possibly pitch a perfect game, watch how carefully the other players do all they can to *not* focus on the potential feat at hand. Other than pitching, bowling, and Olympic competition, few sports or occupations even measure perfection, and yet instinctively we seem determined to pursue it. I say, let's pursue imperfection!

*Our imperfections—and
our ability to deal outside
our comfort zone—are
what truly impress people.*

Instead of fearing what might go wrong, why not embrace it as an opportunity to show others the *real* you?

When things go wrong, we allow observers to see a more intimate and unrehearsed side of us. Typically, such moments cannot be planned for because they often happen organically, but that spontaneous side of ourselves is what many really *want* to see. When we deal with an unforeseen situation, we show others how we behave under pressure in the real world. This lets them see your human side, your true character. Imperfection is relatable.

I once heard a story about actor Richard Harris that truly illustrates this point. He had played the role of King Arthur in *Camelot* countless times in his career. During a performance in his later years, he forgot the words to one of his signature songs. Although the orchestra attempted to cover for him, he signaled them to stop playing. The audience gasped as he walked downstage and said, "I must confess, I have forgotten the words. Perhaps, if it is not too much trouble, you could help me remember them." There wasn't a dry eye in the theater as the audience stood in unison and sang the timeless "Camelot." I am quite sure it was an experience that no one in attendance will ever forget. I wish I had been there.

The pursuit of perfection is a noble cause, but the acceptance of imperfection is a wonderful opportunity to just be you. When you embrace your flaws, you will find that it brings you closer to those around you. Your smile and easygoing attitude will be on display and will win others over—and they'll love you all the more for it!

Fear: **I'm Not as Prepared as I Should Be** *Response:* **Run Your Race**

One of the biggest fears that plagues us all is fear of the unknown. We all deal with the stress of communicating under pressure. Some people excel under pressure, whereas others tend to wither and weaken under the weight of it. We often read about tips and ideas to help battle this nemesis—and I will provide some food for thought—but I believe that the battle is won before you make the call, appear onscreen, or walk into a room.

Repetition is the greatest friend of all who struggle to believe in themselves. The more we put ourselves in stressful situations, the easier it becomes to cope. But even familiarity can cause problems because we can be lured into complacency. Do you really want to avoid *all* anxiety before an important meeting or interaction? Be careful what you wish for. I know many successful salespeople who look forward to that slight uneasy feeling before a sales call or presentation. As a matter of fact, the only time such people are nervous is when they feel *nothing* before a meeting. There is an ominous foreboding that this might be the day they perform flatly.

The fact is, we want that pressure; we *need* that pressure, and it's the pressure that makes us unforgettable. We know that the stress will abate a few minutes into the conversation, so it's those first few minutes that are the roughest. Unfortunately, that's when others are judging us the harshest. When I coach others, I focus on working out those first few minutes of conversation because if pressure gets in the way, the powerful opening is lost. That's why we work hard on what happens before a conversation even begins. Consider the following three simple acts to help you manage this or, for that matter, *any* pressure situation: show up early, prepare your mind, and visualize.

Show up early. I mean *early!* I am always amazed when I see someone show up only 30 minutes before a presentation and begin to set up. I show up significantly earlier for a host of reasons: maybe there might be traffic; maybe my directions or navigator is wrong; maybe I'll have trouble finding a place to park. What's the worst that could happen when you show up too early? Nothing—grab a cup of coffee and relax.

Prepare your mind. It is not uncommon for there to be a lot going on before an important conversation.

There might be others you did not plan to meet with
who may have questions, a special request, or a favor
to ask. Before you know it, your name is called, and
you're on. Is that really the way you want to start your
"race"? You show up early so that, at least a few minutes
before go time, you don't have to worry about answering
questions or coping with distractions. Find a quiet area
where there's a comfortable chair or take a short walk to
mentally prepare.

Visualize. It's difficult for me to tell you exactly what
to visualize because that depends on you. Many people
prepare by visualizing the first few statements they
will make or questions they will ask, or by imagining
themselves successfully accomplishing the task at hand.
My mental image is of a racehorse getting ready to run the
track. In my mind, I am walking slowly around a mental
paddock, quiet and at peace, relishing the thought of the
race that's soon to start.

When under pressure, we get caught up in many unnecessary worries that are usually beyond our control. Why
compound your stress by taking your mind to a negative
place? Preparation is the secret weapon—and not just
preparation for the conversation but also for that time
before the conversation. When you are properly prepared,
doesn't it make sense to take your mind to a positive
place? If you're feeling pressure, just remind yourself

that these are the moments in life that make us feel alive. *That* is something you can control!

Enjoy your race. There certainly can be a lot at stake when you step into a pressure situation that tests your nerves—and that's not a bad thing! Believing in yourself is all about having faith in what you do. That doesn't mean constantly talking yourself into and out of various ideas but rather committing to the ideas you already have.

Fear: **I Won't Be Good Enough**
Response: **Trust Yourself**

I can remember a funny time when I forgot to trust myself and the ideas I had or, more accurately, I became bored with them. It started harmlessly enough: I was preparing a presentation for a charity event. I put just enough creative touches into the presentation to make it interesting without taking away from the subject itself. Then I did something I don't recommend, particularly if the goal is to reduce fear: I kept picking at it.

It began with a few extra sound effects. *After all,* I told myself, *adding a couple of sound effects certainly isn't going to ruin the presentation!* Besides, it made me laugh, and if it made me laugh, I knew it would make my audience laugh, too.

Then I began to insert small asides designed to involve the audience. I had a few strategically placed, and I thought they would be magical moments. Because they looked so good, I put in more—a lot more. I figured they would just strengthen the presentation.

Finally, the floodgates opened. I incorporated video, then I inserted multiple fonts, templates, transitions, and other gimmicks (I mean special effects). I even found a 20-foot ladder, like one you'd find in a big box store, which I covered with fabric and strategically placed so that I could dramatically climb it and continue my presentation while towering above the audience from the opposite end of the room. Yes, I was going to take this audience to a place they had never been before! I had a fever: more-is-better-itus.

I was consumed by this newfound illness, which told me to throw at my listeners everything but the kitchen sink. My reward was a confused and detached audience that seemed unable to focus on the content of the presentation. Something was distracting them: me.

Why do we believe that the more we put into something, the better it will be? Was I adding all the bells and whistles to build a better presentation, or was I just using them as a crutch? It's ironic that the more *stuff* we put into what we're doing, the weaker the product becomes. The reason for this is simple: the stuff ultimately gets in the way of the actual content. That stuff can change the look of something, but it isn't going to get people to believe in you. Only mastering what you are doing will win people over.

When you are physically and mentally prepared, look
sharp, and feel ready to go, don't listen to that voice in
your head that nags you to keep adding more stuff. Leave
it out. If you trust yourself, your best will be more than
good enough.

Fear: I'm Just Not That Interesting
Response: Commit to Who You Are

You are who you are. If you're a fairly serious person,
commit to it: be the best fairly serious person you can be.
If you're analytical, commit to that; it doesn't mean you
can't explain something to someone who is more socially
outgoing. If you like to smile, commit to that. You don't
need to try to be someone you're not—just be who you
are. After all, who does a better imitation of you than,
well, you?

Being comfortable in your own skin does wonders to
reinforce the faith that you have in yourself. Humor
is a good example. Many people I work with express
fear because they do not feel particularly funny and are
concerned about how they will be perceived. Humor
comes easily to me. Maybe it's because I used to obses-
sively watch old-time comedians like my personal
favorite, Jerry Lewis, as well as Red Skelton, Jackie
Gleason, George Carlin, Buddy Hackett, Don Rickles,
and Milton Berle, to name a few. Maybe it's just how I'm

genetically programmed. Whatever the reason, I've never had to spend much time thinking about how to be funny.

Unfortunately, when clients have asked me if I can help them be funny, I kind of panic. I've never learned a formula for how to be funny. Some clients have gone so far as to ask me to write jokes for them. I go by this rule of thumb: *If you need to ask me to make you funny, most likely you are not a naturally funny person.* I know that sounds harsh, but you don't have to be funny to believe in yourself or to be a terrific communicator. This is puzzling to some people, so let's demystify the subject of humor and at the same time dispel a few myths.

Humor is the most overrated approach to effective communication.

It is astonishing to me that this statement seems to both confuse and shock people. Some of the greatest orators in history were not considered funny people. They were known for their ability to fascinate and hold the attention of those they spoke to, and humor was not part of the equation. That list includes some of our greatest presidents, leaders, and visionaries, including Barak Obama, Nelson Mandela, Mahatma Gandhi, and, yes, Mr. Rogers—all of whom changed the course of history, and none of whom used humor as a tool.

The question remains: Why do so many people want to be someone they're not when they are communicating with others? It's because they are concerned about gaining and holding other people's attention—and that is a valid concern. I'm not saying that humor isn't an effective approach to gaining interest, but it's way overrated. I'll remind you that there are many ways to accomplish that goal, and most do not include humor! When I work with clients, I present them with more than 25 ways to arouse or sustain people's interest. The clear majority of those tips have nothing to do with humor. The following are just two examples.

Questions Such a fundamental part of communication, and yet so overlooked, just asking questions makes you interesting. In fact, the more questions you ask, and the more the person you are communicating with speaks, the more they enjoy talking with you. You don't need to stress about being a fascinating storyteller; you just need to load up with questions to hear the stories of others.

Nonverbal cues These can take many forms, but the most important nonverbal cues are our gestures and facial expressions. They not only pique interest in your conversations but it has also been proven that the emotional impact of any message is greatly enhanced by a combination of the right words and the right nonverbal cues.

When you use nonverbal cues well—or any other skills that come naturally to you—they are subtle and make you seem relaxed. And the people you are communicating with are often unaware of what you are doing that makes the conversation interesting and enjoyable to them. What they *are* aware of is that they are interested in what you are saying. You don't need to fear not being funny enough or interesting enough. Focus on what comes naturally to you because fear is just not an option.

Fear: **I Can't Control the Actions of Others** *Response:* **Play the Course— Not the Opponent**

I am not much of a golfer. I've just never had the time to work on my golfing skills. When business was strong, I had no time to play. When business was slow, why would I have been playing golf? But I have played the game, at times well, and I respect the sport.

There is an interesting aspect of golf that used to puzzle me: why do professional golfers refuse to look at the scoreboard when they are in competitions? They can play for four days, meticulously keeping track of every shot they take, and yet they seem totally uninterested in how their fellow competitors are doing. If they do take a peek, it won't be until the final hole or two. This isn't something you see just with a quirky player or two. Nearly all the great players do it.

Watch a college or professional basketball coach and you'll see that they *always* watch the scoreboard. Based on what they are seeing, they make adjustments to counteract what the opponent is doing. After all, they need their team to play strategically. It's important that they keep track of what the opponent is up to.

The elite golfers go about it completely differently. To be elite, they must master the physical game at a level many of us cannot even comprehend. But that's only half of what it takes to be an elite golfer: they also must master the mental game. They must quiet their emotions, focus completely, and have total confidence in every swing they take. Would such a mind-set benefit you?

Think about the last time you were prepping for a critical interview or an important meeting with a potential client. What mind-set did you subscribe to? For most, it's that of a typical competitor: you split your time preparing for what you could and could not control. The aspects you could control—like the questions you would ask, the materials you would bring, and your overall preparation and execution—gave you confidence *because* they were 100 percent within your control.

Here's the thing: You also unwittingly devoted a great deal of time to the aspects you could *not* control—things like what your competition might be up to or your competitor's overall preparation and execution. You may have even worried about the politics that might be behind the job or the client you were attempting to land. I suppose that on some level these were legitimate worries, but they were things over which you had absolutely no control, and those worries no doubt contributed mightily to the fear you were feeling. How does worrying about your opponent's performance help *your* performance? It doesn't. Do you now see the genius behind the elite golfers' mind-set?

Control what you *can* control: *your* game, *your* preparation, *your* execution. Play the course to the best of your ability and don't be distracted by your opponents. With that mind-set, you can quiet your emotions and focus intently on what you are there to do. You will be able to perform at your optimal level and control whatever fear may be nagging you. What else can you hope for?

Fear is not something that can be wished away or conquered by some Jedi mind trick. Fear lives in all of us, but that doesn't mean it can rule us. Often fear is based on irrational thought, and such thoughts can just as easily be reversed by logic. It's logical to accept fear as an instinct, and it's just as logical to accept that fear can be managed with reason.

CHAPTER

3

Getting Others to Believe You

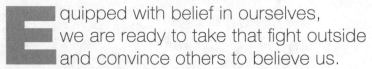 quipped with belief in ourselves, we are ready to take that fight outside and convince others to believe us. On the surface it seems so easy to get others to believe us, and for some lucky individuals it is—for a time. But rest assured, there isn't a soul on this earth who hasn't questioned their ability to be believed. As a matter of fact, many of us are just one brutal rejection away from questioning all that we are.

That last statement wasn't made to depress you; it was made to encourage you. No one is impervious to doubt, and that's why building a measurable process to use when seeking the belief of others is so important. It validates what we do on our good days and problem-solves what we do on our not-so-good days.

It Is Not What You Know That Makes People Believe You

How is it that so many of us are misled into thinking that the more we know, the more credibility we have and the more we will be believed? It can be humbling to stand in front of an individual or a group and realize that they may ask questions that you can't answer. I've pulled out many a yellow pad and proclaimed, "I don't know everything, but I do know where to find the answers to everything!" No one expects you to be a fact machine; they know you are human—just like them.

The problem is, do something enough and unfortunately you may never have to pull out that yellow pad again. I say "unfortunately" because your knowing everything can cause frustration in others, which can turn to distrust; that distrust often turns to cynicism, and sometimes that cynicism even turns to aggressive behavior—and for what? Knowing too much?

This may sound strange, but people trust those who have the courage to admit when they don't know something. And once someone admits that, it builds trust in the answers they *can* provide. Professing to know everything is delivering a flawed message that ultimately undermines the trust others have in you.

I have worked with some big-name professional speakers who have, from time to time, been known to break one of the most critical rules of public speaking: they will lie. When they hear the second or third difficult question from an analytical audience, they will pause, furrow their brow, and say, "That's a terrific question. I believe the answer is [x], but let me double-check and get back to you."

Instantly, you can see the audience heave a collective sigh of relief. I'm not advocating for dishonesty, and it seems absurd that we are perceived as more truthful when we don't know all the answers, but these professional speakers are well aware that coming across as a know-it-all is off-putting and can undermine their credibility. You don't need to stand in front of a group of smart people to learn this simple lesson.

Author Edward Abbey wrote in *Desert Solitaire,* "There is a way of being wrong which is also sometimes necessarily right." Those are wise words when it comes to capitalizing on opportune moments to earn the trust of others. There is a key difference between those who struggle to get others to believe them and those who don't: People who lack confidence obsess about the unknown. Those who are confident not only accept it but embrace it.

Find Your Communication Rhythm

There is a definite rhythm to effective communication, and mastering that meter will do wonders in getting others to believe you. Interestingly enough, the first time I became aware of this phenomenon was at the age of 16, when I started working.

My first job was as an usher at Roth's Seven Locks Movie Theatre in Potomac, Maryland. I proudly wore my red-and-black blazer and manned my flashlight like a pro. Leaning on the back wall of the theater, I also saw a lot of movies.

It was a tremendous experience because after I'd had my fill of watching the same movie repeatedly, I began watching the audience. I could see only the backs of their heads, of course, but that taught me plenty. During an intense part of the movie, no one moved a muscle; when the intensity broke, so did everyone's attention. As if on cue, hundreds of people would simultaneously shift in their seats, stretch, or reach for popcorn or a beverage. If the movie was a good one, it wouldn't be long before the audience was once again totally engaged and motionless.

The ebb and flow of the action created a rhythm, and each movie's writer and director had calculated and carefully orchestrated the rhythm they wanted you to feel. Too much intensity would wear the audience out; they would grow numb to the message and lose interest. Too little action would put everyone to sleep. But the right mix of intensity and relief would thrill the audience, and they would stay glued to their seats.

Such rhythm is also part of how we communicate with one another. We all try to inject power and energy into the words we speak. If you sustain a level of intensity in every word you say, it will captivate the people you are speaking to—at first—but in time you'll lose them. Your communication partners will become restless and irritated, and the words that at first seemed exciting and melodic will morph into an annoying squawk. Worst of all, the critical points of your message will be lost because no one will know where to find them.

Hollywood writers and directors understand what they want you to feel through the words and actions in their movies. They know what message they want you to remember and what songs they want you to hum as you exit the theater. When you communicate with others, you are both writer and director of your own movie. What do you want others to feel and remember when you speak? Once you define the core message you want to convey, there are several ways to help others find it:

▶ You can slow down your voice to draw people in.

▶ You can speed up your voice to hold their attention.

▶ You can add emphasis to highlight a point.

▶ You can add nonverbal cues to intensify your message.

Choose your moments and change up your vocal delivery and you will take a major leap forward in getting others to believe you. Just keep an eye on your pitch and pace—and learn to leverage the power of the pause.

Use the Power of the Pause

As a society we just don't seem to like silence! We do just about anything to avoid it. We spend hours preparing for conversations, just to make sure there won't be any uncomfortable silences. We talk when we have nothing to say. We even throw in filler words like "um" and "uh" to make sure there isn't a moment of silence between our words. Here's the irony: pauses can be one of the most powerful communication tools at our disposal.

There are three ways to verbally communicate: we can make statements, we can ask questions, and we can listen. Of those three, it's been proven time and again:

Asking questions and listening are the two most important ways to communicate.

Sounds simple enough, but what happens if we put our phobia of silence together with our need to ask questions and listen? In a sense, that is a recipe for a perfect storm or, I should say, a perfect *bad communication* storm. We know we must ask questions to get others to believe us and to stay in control of a conversation, but questions are ineffective if you can't convince the other person that you are honestly listening to their answers.

Here are a few scenarios you might recognize.

▶ To stay in control, we frequently try to figure out our next question before the other person has finished answering our first one. We risk not only missing valuable information but also demonstrating just how poorly we listen by asking a question that has just been answered.

▶ Even if we *are* in the moment and focused, we may literally be squirming for an opportunity to ask more questions rather than experience a moment of silence. If we have posed a good query—perhaps a deep, probing one—we need to be listening to and processing the answer rather than quickly responding with a follow-up question.

It seems so obvious. Why don't we just pause more? The answer is quite simple: pausing a conversation is not nearly as easy as it might seem.

One of the biggest reasons why the pause is so difficult is because of our own internal clock. I use the term *clock* metaphorically because our internal clocks don't use the same unit of measure as an actual timepiece. In fact, it's a faster clock. If you don't believe me, sit down with a friend and time the pauses you *think* you're taking in your conversation. We are so uncomfortable with silence that our internal clock runs about three times faster than an actual clock. What feels like three seconds to you is actually about one second in real time.

If the person you were speaking to was using *your* internal clock, I'd let this point go, but they use a *real* clock! What feels like a few seconds to you is a split second to the other person, so they feel like you haven't heard a word they've said. If the other person thinks you aren't listening, they certainly aren't going to find what you are saying credible.

Imagine a conversation that goes like this:

You: If it isn't too much trouble, I'd sure like to hear about that.

Person A: I've never told anyone this before, but that part of my life worries me.

You [in a split second]: Why do you feel that way?

Can you see how disingenuous that follow-up question would feel to the other person? For years I have battled this problem with clients, using a secret weapon: a metronome. I devise scenarios that require deep, sometimes painful questions, and I allow those questions to be asked and answered. I set the metronome to a nice, easy beat, and when a response to a question is delivered, I have my clients wait three beats before responding in any way. It can feel like an agonizingly long pause, when in reality it's rarely longer than three seconds. How do we make the best use of those three seconds?

▶ With eye contact

▶ With facial expressions that mirror those of the other person

▶ With an expression that shows that we are actively listening and concentrating on what was said

▶ With a demonstration of empathy that comes naturally when we are truly processing the words we've just heard

When you allow yourself to experience the power of the pause, you will find yourself connecting at a deeper level with other people and becoming a lot more believable to them. It might require a metronome, or perhaps just a good sense of rhythm, but with a little discipline we can all get there.

It's not the words that often betray us but rather the spaces between them.

Develop a Communication Shot Clock

Professional basketball is a fast-paced game. One reason why is because the players are forced to shoot the ball within a set time, as measured by the shot clock. One eye is frequently on the opponent, and the other is on the clock. This keeps the game moving, keeps it exciting, and helps hold our attention. Wouldn't it be interesting if there were a communication shot clock? If there were, it would sure help our ability to be believed!

I was a lucky kid for many reasons, one of which was my dad, Lee Jolles, who taught me many amazing things. One of the best things I learned was something he didn't even realize he was teaching me. Like most parents, my dad always asked about my day. He would pull up a chair, look me in the eye, and lock on to whatever words of mine would follow—for about 45 seconds. Then he would drift away, first mentally and then physically. As a child, that didn't make me feel great, but his actions taught me this immensely important communication tactic. Either consciously or unconsciously, he was using the communication shot clock.

We live in a society that demands that we pick up the pace on just about everything we do, particularly how we communicate. Emails are faster, books are smaller, tweets are a limited number of characters, and blogs are more succinct. Each form of communication attempts to achieve the same goal: to hold the viewer's attention. After all, if you can't hold another person's interest, you will struggle to be believed.

I think my dad would have been thrilled with the fast-paced communication environment we live in. He wanted his information quickly, and he wanted the most significant parts identified. Perhaps most importantly, if he wanted to learn more, he'd ask.

As a five-year old, I may have tended to ramble when I communicated, but as an eight-year-old I no longer did. I learned how to address a question, provide an intriguing answer, and finish my response unrushed—all in 45 seconds or less. People believed what I was saying and acted on it. Rather than offer multiple examples of a given point, I learned to provide my best example. Rather than try to guess which part of a story others might like the best, I'd let them decide. Rather than guess how long I should speak, I had my own internal clock.

A communication shot clock can be applied to many scenarios.

▶ When we want others to believe us and it's our turn to talk, we don't need to ramble on about an idea. We need to succinctly tie the needs of those we are speaking with to the value our idea provides.

▶ When we are in an interview, we don't need to go on about ourselves. We need to specifically tie the needs of the employer to the strengths that we bring to the table.

▶ When we write, we don't need to elaborate at length about a specific point. We need to be precise and provide value to those who have been gracious enough to read our words.

If we choose our words carefully, our communication shot clock can be set to 45 seconds. What's more, when we work with a communication shot clock, we eliminate the guesswork of trying to determine what would be most interesting to our listener. Instead, we simply present a succinct message and let the listener decide what they find most interesting. Their response will let us know what they want to hear more about.

My dad may have been tough on me as a child, but I am immensely grateful that he taught me the value of communication that is crisp and to the point. Guess what happens when you are crisp and to the point? Yep—you become more believable.

Embrace Dysfunction

I respect anyone who meticulously prepares to do their very best, no matter what the task. I certainly expect that same preparation from my doctor, my lawyer, my accountant, and the many other people I count on. I also expect that same level of preparation from any client I am coaching—but that doesn't mean we should be bothered by moments that are less than perfect.

Some years ago I watched a colleague conduct a workshop for an insurance company. He was about to do an exercise designed to track a recent buying decision a volunteer had made. There were about 300 people in the audience, and when the presenter asked for a volunteer, one brave soul raised his hand. The man awkwardly admitted that he had recently purchased a car. My colleague had a scribe ready to go onstage as he moved into the audience toward the volunteer. With a microphone in hand, he began asking a series of questions he had prepared. The first question was the easiest, and the banter that followed reminded me of a courtroom scene from the movie *My Cousin Vinny* (1992) around actor Joe Pesci's pronunciation of the word *youth*.

The exchange went something like this:

> PRESENTER: "What car did you buy?"

> VOLUNTEER: "A 2-ton dually."
> [in a deep southern drawl]

> PRESENTER: "A what?"
> [some laughter]

> VOLUNTEER: "A 2-ton dually."

> PRESENTER: "Uh, what was that word?"
> [more laughter]

> VOLUNTEER: "What word?"

> PRESENTER: "Did you say, 'a 2-ton dually'?"
> [even more laughter]

> VOLUNTEER: "Yeah, a 2-ton dually."

> PRESENTER: "What is a 2-ton dually?!"
> [yet more laughter]

The howls of the audience let us all know how much
they loved seeing their presenter squirm! Over the next
10 minutes, the volunteer and the presenter moved
through a kind of rhythmic dance. The man was throwing
words at the presenter that he had never heard before, and
the presenter was trying diligently to gather the information he needed to make the exercise work. But I could also
see that the presenter was feigning a level of confusion
and a lack of knowledge in this particular area of auto

mechanics. In the end, the man gave the presenter *exactly* what he was looking for. For the audience, however, it looked like the volunteer made the presenter work hard for it—and therein lies the magic.

That exercise was only a small part of the workshop, but it was all the participants wanted to talk about when the session was over. When the presenter spoke to the client who had hired him to conduct the workshop, that was all *she* wanted to talk about, as well. When the presenter bumps into people—years later—who had been in that audience, that is *still* all they want to talk about.

People don't remember content as much as they remember the experience.

If you're wondering why so many people continued to ask about that workshop, it's because its presenter was rehired to conduct many more workshops. The client liked that first presentation so much that she hired the presenter for five more years of training.

When he goes to the client's training facility, my colleague hears this every time: "How about that 2-ton dually guy! He really got you, didn't he?!"

Each time he hears it, he responds in the same way and with the same sheepish grin: "He sure did!"

The greatest way to earn the respect of an audience or any individual is *not* to demonstrate how much you know or how able you are to perform what was planned. The way to earn that respect is to demonstrate your agility in those moments that are clearly *not* planned.

> *People don't want to see how perfect you are; they want to see how human you are.*

Does this mean we should plan for dysfunctional moments in a presentation or conversation? No. It means we can embrace moments that are clearly unplanned, and we can learn to relax and go with them. Doing so may very well take us on an authentic, unscripted journey that will not only help others believe what they are hearing but provide those moments of communication that are truly unforgettable.

Pay Attention to Transitions

When you want to be believed, presenting a thought or an idea can be a little tricky. We tend to obsess about the message itself but pay little attention to how we get to those thoughts or ideas and how we move off those thoughts or ideas. Watch a good performer and you'll see what I mean—and you don't have to see that performer live; just listen to a live recording.

As far back as I can remember, I've always liked buying live-recorded music: live albums, eight-tracks, cassettes, CDs, and downloads. I love the music, and I love listening to the performer. I like live music because it allows me to *believe* the music.

One of my favorite live recordings, which I still love to listen to, is RCA's *An Evening with John Denver.* Recorded in 1974 and released in 1975, the music is just amazing. Denver performed it live, and both the songs and the music are wonderful. When Denver sang, we believed him. But *why* did we believe him?

▶ Was it the actual songs he wrote and sang? They were beautiful but quite simple.

▶ Was it his voice? Again, he had a beautiful voice, but there are others with better voices with richer tones.

So, what was it? I think it was the things he shared between songs. I enjoyed those moments every bit as much, if not more, than the songs themselves. When Denver would tell you what he was thinking, doing, or feeling, it didn't change the sounds he was making when he sang, but it changed our perception of his music. It made us believe.

It is such ad-libs—those spontaneous reactions to what
is around us, those improvisational moments that cannot
be scripted or prepared for—that truly make someone
believable. It's strangely ironic: often the more we rehearse
and strive for perfection, the less believable we are.

Now that we understand the need for transitions in and
around our messages, it's time to move to the final transition: a transition to a strong finish, or what I refer to as a
"transition out."

Transition out I unconsciously stumbled on this transition during a radio interview with a host who is almost
as intense as I am. Because we weren't in the same studio,
the host couldn't see me as I spoke, so he had no idea
when I was done with my answers to his questions. As a
result, he would frequently talk over me because he didn't
want dead air if I had finished speaking. To address this,
I began providing a transition; I slowed down a bit and
lowered my voice while wrapping up my response:

> So you see, Jim, to protect that investment, we aren't
> really treating this event as a training session. We're
> treating it as a cultural change within your organiza-
> tion, and I'm going to be here to make sure you are
> able [begin slowing down and dropping voice here]
> to
>
>   do
>
>   just
>
>   that.

There's a level of personal style applied to this response, and the personality of the individual you are communicating with certainly needs to be factored in, but the important pieces are in place. There's a transition into your message, a better-thought-out transition around the words you are putting forth, and then a transition out with a voice drop for the slower final few words. This technique works beautifully to make you more believable because you are punctuating your message with your delivery and driving your point home.

It is natural to focus on the body of your message, and doing so enables you to effectively convey information. That's good, but it doesn't necessarily make you more believable. When you can transition in and around your message, and then have a transition out, you've just moved your answer from good to great.

Remember: Listening Beats Talking

When you are on your game, you should be speaking roughly as much as you are listening. That's not in question anymore, nor is it a mystery. What *is* in question is how many people actually *succeed* at listening as much they speak.

If you ask people why they like to talk, they'll probably tell you that it gives them a sense of control in the conversation. How many times have you heard an individual who was nervously preparing for a business meeting, or even a first date, say, "I've got to figure out what I'm going to say!" What to *say*? If I'm going to prepare for an encounter, I'd spend my time figuring out the *questions* to ask.

The person who is talking is usually **not** the one controlling the conversation.

I frequently use smartphones to prove to people that though they may *think* they are listening as much as they are speaking, in fact they were not. I've misled groups (yes, professional speakers do this from time to time) and told them I was looking to measure their communication style. When they are asked to count the number of statements versus questions and hear ratios of 10-to-1 and even 20-to-1, the point is loud and clear.

I will concede that asking questions is not an instinctive behavior. Asking questions is not easy—it takes work—but it's a skill all who desire to communicate more effectively must master. Once you do, you're in a perfect position to do something that seems to have stumped most of mankind: listen.

There is not a soul on this earth who at some point doesn't struggle with their ability to get others to believe them.

But getting others to believe you does not depend on some special gene you need to be born with. It requires a commitment and, when you get knocked down, the discipline to get up and try again.

4

Stepping Up Your Game

The principles behind becoming believable to others are straightforward, yet so many struggle with them. That's because there is so much more involved than just learning a process. Getting people to believe you requires work. It requires patience, it requires determination, and it requires that you step up your game. The words make up a process, but "this" makes it so much more. What exactly is "this," you might ask? It's a great question!

"This" Makes All the Difference

Some time ago I was reminiscing about one of my favorite television commercials; it's a FedEx ad referred to as "The Stolen Idea" that can be viewed on YouTube. It takes place in a conference room, with a team of executives looking for ideas to cut costs. One guy floats what seems like a good idea. After a pause and no reaction from the group, the boss presents the same exact idea. When the group celebrates the boss's idea, the frustrated guy who came up with it says: "You just said the same thing I said—only you did *this*," and he gestures with his hands.

The boss replies: "No, I did *this*," and he gestures in a slightly different way. Everyone at the table agrees with the boss and congratulates him, and the commercial ends.

When you Google "FedEx Stolen Idea," you'll see a lot written about this commercial, and most of it isn't good. It's not the ad that gets blasted but the fact that credit is often not given to those who deserve it. I believe there's a completely different message that's being missed. Watch the commercial again and this time focus on the individual who initially presents his idea, noting his manner. His idea is a good one, but he delivers it in a hesitant way that lacks confidence. Although his words convey a good idea, they are defeated by his uninspired and passionless delivery.

Now watch the boss and see how he does more than just repeat the words. He *sells* those words through his pitch, tone, facial expressions, gestures, and body language. The boss uses the power of the pause, then corrects the employee and points out how he gestured and spoke in a different way—and the first thing you'll hear from those around him is "It makes all the difference." And they are right.

"This" happens to be a critical part of any message we deliver. Albert Mehrabian's 7-38-55 rule of personal communication provides a framework for analyzing the commercial. Originally pertaining only to feelings and attitudes (and widely misinterpreted), the 7-38-55 rule posits that 7 percent of the emotional impact of a message comes from the words we use; that's the part we hear delivered by the employee in the commercial. But words alone do not convince: 55 percent of the emotional impact of a message comes from body language, which you see in the boss's performance. The remaining 38 percent of the impact comes from the pitch and tone of the voice, the speed and rhythm of the words, and the power of the pause—or "this."

You don't have to see someone face-to-face to feel the impact of their delivery. It's been said that you can hear a smile. Don't believe it? Try taking the voicemail test: Leave a one-minute message for yourself the way you normally talk. Then leave the same voicemail while standing up, smiling, and speaking as though the person were in front of you. Now play them back. Which message portrays you best?

Whether you are a salesperson, a manager, a presenter, a parent, or someone just trying to get others to believe in your idea—if you want your words to carry weight, you need to learn how to do "this." Once you do, you'll be farther down the path to being believed and moving those around you to do "that"!

Don't believe that the tune is as important as the words? Look no further than the rise of Donald Trump. No matter what your political views might be, you must admire the level of confidence he wields when he speaks to a friendly crowd. After one of his many controversial statements during the presidential campaign, he smugly stated, "I could stand in the middle of Fifth Avenue and *shoot* somebody [gesturing with his hand as with a gun] and I wouldn't lose voters!" It's no coincidence that he typically struggles to read from a monitor. The words are there for him, but the tune is not. But when he, and others like him, can mix the words and the tune together, you are bound to see and hear something far more authentic and believable.

When you consider the power of "this" and the tune with which we speak, it may seem like the words aren't all that important. That isn't true. They are important because the words and the tune, when taken together, are greater than the sum of the parts. As the saying goes, it's not just what you say; it's how you say it.

It's Not What People Hear; It's What They Feel

By now you're well aware of my contention that words are overvalued. I am guiltier than most of leaning on words. I teach people how to foster trust by using the correct words. I teach them how to ask questions. I show people how to persuade, influence, perform, and generally communicate on all levels using the appropriate words. I've been told I'm pretty good with words, but sometimes I forget to remind my clients that words can be meaningless if they are spoken without conviction.

One of my favorite stories that I relate in seminars illustrates this point. Mark Twain was known for many things, one of which was his propensity to swear. This evidently annoyed his wife to no end. One day while shaving, the story goes, he nicked himself and let out a healthy stream of curse words. In the other room, his wife was so incensed that she proceeded to write down every word he uttered. When he entered the room, she read them all back to him. He listened attentively, smiled, and supposedly said, "That's very good, honey. You've got the words; you just don't know the tune."

Think for a moment about *your* tune.

- ▶ When you ask someone to tell you their story, does your tune say you sincerely care?

- ▶ When you ask someone to tell you their concerns, does your tune say you feel true empathy?

- ▶ When you ask someone to trust you, does your tune encourage that person to believe you?

- ▶ When you ask someone to have faith in you, does your tune imply that you are worthy of their faith?

It's not just the words that matter but how you say them. But let's go deeper. How exactly do you carry the correct tune? It's right there in front of you.

Just Tell the Truth

The struggle to be believed and to find the correct tune can be mighty, but one of the most effective solutions is right there in front of us: tell the truth. To be believable, you *must* tell the truth. Take a moment and think about that: the easiest way to be believable is to tell the truth.

After all, the only person who knows if you are—or are not—telling the truth is you.

If you don't believe in what you are saying, it's not the words that will betray you—it's the tune. Not telling the truth is like playing a musical instrument and all the notes are flat. When people aren't speaking the truth, the facial expressions are slightly forced and their nonverbal cues are out of sync with their words. The harder they work to unnaturally adjust these "tells," the more obvious their disingenuous delivery becomes.

This holds true when you are looking for someone to believe in an idea, in a product, or even in you as a person. If you believe it, your tune will support it. Even those overrated words we cling to will be more effortlessly available.

That means if you feel that the company, product, or idea you represent isn't what it should be, focus your time and energy on improving it. If you feel *you* aren't what you should be, focus your time and energy on improving *you*. I understand that finding a fix can be complex, but sometimes half the battle is leaving your comfort zone, pursuing change, and seeking a solution that is often well overdue. Once you do, the truth will be on your side, and your credibility will be right there with it.

*It isn't nearly as difficult to ask someone to believe you when **you** believe you.*

You don't have to overthink this, or overact, or even act at all. Simply tell the truth, and your words will naturally sync with your tune. You'll be one step closer to conveying the authentic sound you are seeking. Those you are communicating with won't just hear your words, they'll *feel* them—and believe them—too.

Say It Like You Mean It!

I am guessing that most of us had some interesting part-time jobs when we were growing up. I know I had my fair share. One of my more unusual and challenging jobs was during my senior year of high school, when I worked as an umpire with my best friend Bob Haller; we umpired dozens of games together.

I envied Bob because he was 6 inches taller than me and about 50 pounds heavier; his voice was quite a bit lower than mine, so when he made a call, no one questioned it. Because of my shorter stature and less forceful voice, when I made a call *everyone* questioned it. Bob and I used the same four words—*strike, ball, out,* and *safe*—yet we had completely different results.

STEPPING UP YOUR GAME   77

During one particularly ugly game, I was dressed down
multiple times by both coaches for making calls they
disagreed with. I went home discouraged and told my
dad that I wanted to quit. He seemed puzzled because
he knew I was a student of the game and took what I did
seriously. When I told him about the hammering I was
taking from the coaches, he asked me to demonstrate how
I made a call. Nervously, I got into my umpire crouch,
pretended to be watching a play, raised my arm in the air,
and said, "out."

He looked at me and told me that he didn't need to
hear any more. He asked me to try it again, only this time
to say it louder. I once again assumed the position and
said, "*out!*"

His look told me all I needed to know: he wasn't pleased.
I could see the Marine in him take over as he sternly told
me to say it again, only louder. "OUT!" I shouted.

Then he shouted right back: "*Are you sure?!*"

I made the mistake of saying yes, but after the look he shot
me, I quickly cleared my voice and shouted, "YES!"

He wasn't through with me, as he shouted, "*ARE YOU
SURE?!*"

I shouted right back: "YES! *OUT!*"

Smiling, he put his hand on my shoulder and said, "If
you make every close call with that volume and level of

conviction, you won't have any more issues with coaches. I can promise you: they won't question the calls you make." Sure enough, they never did again.

I'm not trying to help you become a better umpire but rather to speak with conviction appropriate to your message. There are moments of truth every day, and they require a level of authority that needs to be conveyed with your words, as well as your delivery of those words. When someone asks you if you can do a certain job, they aren't just looking for "Yes, I can do it" whispered back or "YES, I CAN DO IT!" shouted back. They are looking for those words stated with power and conviction of character—they want you to say it like you mean it.

The words may open the door to others' believing you, but the tune helps you pass through it.

Remember: the easiest way to get others to believe what you say is for you to believe it yourself. That means having the courage to believe in yourself when the odds are stacked against you. We all have a negative voice inside that tells us, "Stop! This isn't going to work!" What will you do when you hear that voice?

Find Your Real Voice

Are you aware that most of us unconsciously use different-sounding voices, depending on the situation in which we find ourselves? It starts at an early age, with something as simple as volume control. When you were little and you got too loud, you were admonished to use your "inside voice."

For a firsthand, close-up peek at this multiple-voice phenomenon, take a flight somewhere. You'll find yourself having a pleasant conversation with a flight attendant, who seems perfectly normal—until they pick up the intercom to make announcements. Then you'll hear some weird, mechanical delivery that defies all logic. This bizarre "microphone-inflection voice" is usually delivered with a robotic tone that sounds anything but authentic.

For some reason, the idea of making a public announcement seems to encourage the individual to use a mechanical, singsong voice, emphasizing words like prepositions that are never stressed in normal conversation. No one speaks with those odd inflections when a microphone is *not* in use. Did someone convince flight attendants that a disingenuous voice is easier to understand or more authoritative? Perhaps, but I'm not buying it.

For many, the inside voice and the microphone-inflection voice are just part of their repertoire. There is another, "singsong-presenter voice" that likes to be heard. This voice is notable for an unusual rising and falling rhythm that sounds silly, oversimplified, and insincere—and it can be dangerous for a presenter. This peculiar voice comes across as condescending and can lead an audience to believe that the speaker is talking down to them.

People you are working to communicate with will forgive a lot of voices. They'll forgive a slightly-shaky-nervous voice, or a we-need-to-turn-up-the-microphone voice, or even a stern-in-charge voice, but the condescending singsong-presenter voice can distract and even offend an audience and, in some situations, turn them against the speaker. So how do we stay out of trouble? By remembering two things.

Remember. You don't need to try on new voices because the correct voice has been there all along! The voice you are looking for is your "conversation voice"—the one you use naturally when talking with your friends. Surprised? Don't be. Just because you find yourself addressing a group, other than slowing down just a tick, you don't need to change a thing. The audience wants to hear from you: the conversation you—not the singsong-presenter you. What's more, when an audience feels like they've heard the genuine you, they'll bond faster and tighter with you and believe what you are saying.

Remember to remember. Most speakers are unaware that they use a singsong-presenter voice, as it is an unconscious behavior. Using your natural voice isn't difficult to do—but it can be difficult to keep doing. To prevent you from slipping into an inauthentic voice, simply place a sticky note with the word *conversation* above any speaking notes you have before you. This reminder will give you a mental poke every time you peek at your notes and will be all the reminder you need to stay in your authentic conversation voice.

Falling into a disingenuous voice at the wrong time and with the wrong audience can make for a long day—for you *and* them. This is not about teaching yourself to be someone you aren't; it's about remembering who you are and how you sound when you're with people with whom you are comfortable.

Remembering to use your conversation voice might initially take a prompt or two when you're giving a presentation, but it will be one of the easiest and most powerful fixes you can make. When you use your natural voice, you are being authentic—and that's what every speaker must be before they are believed. Trusting in what you say, saying it like you mean it, and using the voice you use with friends is the best way to be believable to any who are listening.

Understand Your Character

Maybe this all seems a bit overwhelming. After all, I'm asking you to mix the words with the tune and say it like you mean it in your real voice! Wouldn't it be wonderful

if all of this did not require conscious thought and became
effortless? It can. We just need to go to acting school
for a bit.

Although I've spent more than 30 years in front of
audiences, it wasn't until my junior year in high school
that I first formally took to the stage. I was fortunate to
have an amazing teacher and director, Rob Ramoy, who
one day stopped me in the hallway and I told me I *had* to
audition for a show he was directing. The show was *Damn
Yankees* (1955), a musical comedy by George Abbott
and Douglass Wallop. I saw it as an opportunity to play
the role of a baseball player on my favorite team—the
Washington Senators—but I didn't know it would awaken
in me a love for performing and being onstage, and I
certainly didn't realize that it would teach me an invaluable lesson in both acting and being believable.

After a few tense days of auditioning, I was cast as Benny
Van Buren, the manager of the Washington Senators.
I was as green an actor as you could get, and being cast as
a cranky old man certainly didn't make things any easier.
I had no trouble learning my lines, but I just could not
connect with my character. Mr. Ramoy knew I was struggling, so he started pestering me with some of the oddest
questions I could have imagined.

"What kind of car does your character drive?" he asked.
"What kind of car?"

I thought, *Are you kidding me—how would I know **that**?!*

Mr. Ramoy was relentless, and day after day he pressed
on: "What kind of cereal does he eat? What kind of
house does he live in? What type of music does he like?"
I couldn't figure out how in the world this would make
me a better actor, but after some nervous laughter I made
up some answers. It seemed like a waste of time, but if it
made my director happy—and got him off my back—I
figured I'd give it a try.

Every time he passed me in the hall or cornered me
during rehearsal, he'd fire more questions at me. I'm not
sure when it happened, but soon I didn't have to think
hard to give him an answer. It became effortless. Mr.
Ramoy had eventually guided me from playing the role of
the character I was assigned to *being* that character. I was
no longer just reciting lines—I was *believing* the words
I was saying. I walked like my character; I sat like my
character; I *was* my character. If you saw me onstage as
Van Buren, you believed me. It didn't come from the lines
I had memorized but from the persona I had assumed.

Fast-forward a few years, and for the first time I tapped
into my "character" in business. I was interviewing
for New York Life, and I had to pass a personality test.
Before I took it, I asked my prospective manager a simple
question: "Do you want me to answer these questions as
Rob Jolles or as an insurance salesman?"

He laughed and said, "There is absolutely no way to fool this test, so just try to answer it one way or another. Just answer the questions, Jolles!" So I did.

When the results came back, I was called into the manager's office. Right away I could tell that the test hadn't gone well. In a somber tone, he informed me that I had received one of the lowest scores he had ever seen and that he was unable to hire me. I mumbled that I should have taken the test as an insurance salesman. He heard me and told me again that there was no way to fool the test and get a higher score. I didn't disagree with him, but I begged him to let me take the test one more time, and I promised him that I would pass.

A week later I was taking the test again, but this time I got in character: I ate like an insurance salesman, I walked like an insurance salesman, and I dressed like an insurance salesman. Every answer I gave came very easily to me because, for that moment in time, I *was* an insurance salesman. I didn't just pass the test—I received the highest score ever recorded in the Washington office.

My friend Brian Tracy once wrote in his blog, "Whatever you believe, with feeling, becomes your reality."

When you want to be believed, you need to believe with feeling, and learning your character helps you do just that. Companies train people to master the product knowledge—but that's just handing people scripts; they never train people to be the *character* they need to portray. In the end, you may know your lines, but that doesn't mean you will be believed.

Do you see the problem? Do you understand the ramifications of not knowing your character? Can you see the value in understanding your character so that you can deliver your lines with conviction?

We are halfway there. Now let's jump into techniques for learning your character and making you more convincing when it's your turn to make people believe.

Who is your favorite actor? I've always been a fan of Daniel Day-Lewis. Watch him in a movie, and he'll make you believe in whatever character he is playing. He's famous for the intensity with which he studies each of the characters he portrays.

Here are a handful of examples:

- *Lincoln* **(2012)** Day-Lewis insisted that everyone, including his director, Steven Spielberg, refer to him as "Mr. President." For fear that it might throw him off, he would not allow British cast members to speak to him in their natural accents while he was trying to get Abe's voice right.

- *Gangs of New York* **(2002)** For his role as William "Bill the Butcher" Cutting, Day-Lewis took lessons as an apprentice butcher. He was so immersed in the role that he refused to wear a warm jacket because, according to him, it wasn't in keeping with the

period, 1863. He caught pneumonia but rejected
modern medicine when it was offered to him.

▶ *In the Name of the Father* (1993) To accurately
portray wrongly convicted prisoner Gerry Conlon,
Day-Lewis spent several nights at a time chilling in
solitary confinement in the abandoned Irish prison
in which they were filming. He even kept himself
awake for three days in preparation for an interroga-
tion scene.

▶ *The Last of the Mohicans* (1992) To prepare for his
role as Nathaniel "Hawkeye" Poe, Day-Lewis learned
how to hunt animals for food and taught himself
survivalist skills. He refused to eat anything that
he hadn't killed with either his flintlock rifle or his
tomahawk—both of which he could use very well.

▶ *My Left Foot* (1989) While portraying poet Christy
Brown, who suffered from cerebral palsy, Day-Lewis
refused to leave his wheelchair for the entire shoot
and had crewmembers carry him around the set. He
also insisted that he be spoon-fed all of his meals.

Day-Lewis does far more than just learn his lines—he
immerses himself into the life and behaviors of each
character he plays. He is 100 percent believable not just
by learning his lines but by becoming the characters
he portrays.

What about you? How much research do *you* do before you meet with a client? I'm not referring to just visiting their website. I mean *really* researching the client. What are the core values of the individual and the company? Do you know the individual's hobbies or any outside organizations they belong to? What is the client looking for from you? Clearly, the more intensely you research the role you will be playing, the more accurate your character will be. The more time you give to studying the character, the more instinctive and authentic your portrayal.

Once you have a deeper understanding of the company, the personnel, and the scope of work, you can formulate your character. Here's an example: Many younger salespeople are concerned that their age will impede their ability to convince an older client of their competence. Unconsciously, their character is anxious and defensive, and the client perceives that as inexperience, so it becomes a self-fulfilling prophecy.

What if the same young salesperson looked at their age in a different way? What if they defined their character as a person who was innovative, understood cutting-edge technology, and had access to a wide network of personnel and solutions? And what if, deep in that salesperson's soul, they truly believed this? Every move they made and every word they spoke would be supported by this competent young character—someone who was *not* inexperienced but rather wise beyond their years.

This is what understanding your character is all about: turning knowledge and questions into instinctive behavior. If you can identify the character you want to emulate—and truly become that person—your thought processes and delivery will become less rehearsed and more genuine. What's more, your nonverbal cues will be authentic because of one, fundamental reason that I hope you never forget:

The body doesn't know when the mind is acting.

Some say we are born with the ability to make people believe, and I concede that some of us may have a head start. But you can become believable when you understand what "this" brings to the table. The man in the FedEx commercial may have stolen the idea, but his delivery is what sold it. If you believe in your character, you can *become* that person. When that happens, your thoughts, words, and gestures become instinctive, and you are believed. We can all get there.

5

Putting a Lion in Your Heart

Confidence goes a long way toward becoming more believable, and that confidence is accomplished in stages. It's like assembling a puzzle one piece at a time. One puzzle piece comes from learning to believe in ourselves. Another piece comes from learning how to get others to believe us—and not just learning the words but also the tune and the power of "this." Part of that message can be muted if we don't address the stress that affects these puzzle pieces. There are a lot of uncertainties waiting around the bend, so let's examine the courage it takes to embrace change and pursue the unknown.

The act of believing requires an inherent leap of faith.

The Fog of Fear

If you haven't noticed by now, I'm a film buff. At six years old, I would walk with my brother Richard to the Silver Movie Theatre in Silver Spring, Maryland, and thus began my love of movies. I shared that love with my kids—one of our favorite outings was a trip to the theater. I'm open to almost any kind of movie, and its message is what makes me a fan of a particular film. I believe most writers and directors are trying to tell us something, and one of the best examples of a movie with a powerful message is

Defending Your Life (1991), starring Albert Brooks, who also wrote and directed it. It's one of the best movies I've ever seen. I embrace it because it delivers a simple and poignant message about how we can look at our time on this earth. This message also shines a spotlight on why we must not fear the unknowns behind the risks we take but rather celebrate them.

The movie is a wonderful look at Brooks's vision of death. I know it's a morose theme, but Brooks is a comedian, and he takes a kind and gentle look at a topic that most of us would rather not talk about. The film's version of death is quite simple: Upon our passing, each of us spends a few days analyzing our life in a place called Judgment City. In a courtroom, with a prosecutor and a defender, a number of scenes from each person's life are looked at and discussed. Two judges study the scenes and listen to the prosecution and the defense to determine why the individual behaved the way they did. The judges arrive at a verdict, which determines whether the person moves forward through the universe or goes back to live another life to try to get it right.

What I found most fascinating was the ultimate criterion the judges use to make their determinations. Surprisingly, it has little to do with people's day-to-day activities, how much money they made, or their various accomplishments. The success or failure of our lives comes down to one simple question:

Did we overcome our fears, or did we let fear hold us back?

Take a moment to think about that question. How often in life have you shied away from a decision or activity based solely on fear? Perhaps it was an interview, a conversation, a relationship, a new idea, or a presentation. Often fear can mask itself in creative excuses, twisted logic, and well-timed procrastination.

On the flipside, when we can move through our fears and leave our comfort zone to try something daunting, we are immediately rewarded with a sense of deep satisfaction, which often has little to do with the results of our endeavors. Our psyche is smarter than that. We carry that sense of pride because, by golly, we tried! Unfortunately, the more often we let fear hold us back, the more confident and assertive the voice of resistance becomes. But once we start battling through fear, our newfound confidence stifles that voice.

There are many wonderful moments in the movie, but one line caught my attention. During a conversation with his defender (played by Rip Torn), Brooks questions how fear can be such a determining factor in our lives. Torn looks at him and says, "Fear is like a giant fog. It sits on your brain and blocks everything. Real feelings, true happiness, real joy, they can't get through that fog. But you lift it and, buddy, you're in for the ride of your life."

I'm guessing there's a voice in your head, saying, *Maybe today is the day I push through the fog and finally try to* _____. Why not remove the word *maybe* and just push through that fog? Why not just take the plunge and go for it?

Six Words That Will Calm Your Nerves

When you speak for a living, you get all kinds of questions. One of the most common questions I am asked has to do with conquering stage fright. One of my responses is: "Do anything a few thousand times and you'll no longer fear doing it." That may be a great answer for a professional speaker, but most people will never be under pressure in the same way a few thousand times— nor would they want to be!

So, how can I help someone overcome stage fright who doesn't have the benefit of repetition? I often whisper six words:

The audience is rooting for you.

By audience, I don't necessarily mean a roomful of people, watching you onstage. Your audience may very well be an interviewer, a potential client, or a friend you are meeting.

The audience is rooting for you. Now imagine that what I just said is true. Now imagine that I followed that thought with this one: *Hey, I just spoke to your audience, and they all told me that they hope you do a great job today.* Suspend your disbelief for a moment and honestly ask yourself that if you knew for a fact that this was true, wouldn't you go into that boardroom, onto that stage, or into that social situation with more confidence and less anxiety? Yes? Good! Now all I need to do is prove it to you.

We are often so focused on ourselves and our own needs that we completely forget about the people we are pressured to perform in front of and *their* needs. For decades I have asked people in different audiences many questions, and I've never heard anyone say that they were hoping to get as little information as possible from my presentation. As a matter of fact, I've heard quite the opposite.

▶ I've heard audience members tell me that they didn't want to have their time wasted.

▶ I've heard audience members tell me that they didn't want a presenter who was ill prepared.

▶ I've heard audience members tell me that they didn't want a presenter who was indifferent or didn't care.

In other words, the members of your audience are, in fact, rooting for you to be successful. It isn't because they care so deeply about you but rather because by rooting for you, they are rooting for themselves. It does them no good to root against you! Anchor of *Good Morning America* Robin Roberts explained to *Variety* how she copes with speaking anxiety: "It's about focusing on the fight and not the fright."

You can't rid your life of anxiety, but you *can* control it. Understanding how to cope with it—and how others cope with it—certainly helps. Reminding yourself that your communication partners are rooting for you becomes a matter of focus on what *really* matters.

In my coaching practice, various topics come up, and they invariably fall into two categories: things we can control and things we cannot control. Like looking into a mirror, there's always something that we don't like about ourselves. For example, it's amazing how often age discrimination in the workplace comes up. Unless we discover the Fountain of Youth, there's really nothing we can do about that. So, rather than whine about it, I take a different approach that involves a lot more than just age.

Accept and Embrace Your Shortcomings

Ah, the joy of youth: carefree and without worry—until we land our first real job. Then concerns about age rear their ugly head: *Will clients have trouble responding to me because of my youth? Will clients think my age makes me less qualified for the position I hold? If only I were a little older…* Those sentiments are quite real when we begin our work life.

Then some years pass. One day you wake up no longer concerned about how young you are but rather how *old* you are. For those who are struggling professionally, it can become an obsession. As you walk into an important appointment, you find yourself thinking, *I just know they are going to want someone younger than me!* The irony is if the person you are communicating with wasn't concerned about your age—or any other perceived flaw—before, they are now. That imperfection is what I refer to as a "limp." But consider this:

We **all** walk with a limp.

There are a handful of biblical references to this phrase; however, I have my own take on this notion. We all have weaknesses, and those weaknesses represent our personal limp. Our limp is what makes us human. Oddly enough, I have difficulty trusting anyone who appears to have no limp. Maybe it's because I believe that our unique limp—and our ability to adjust to that limp—is what makes us extraordinary. Anyone without a limp is either an imposter or possesses no compassion for those who do have limps.

Our limp can be any physical or physiological imperfection you'd like to identify, and sadly we often let it hold
us back. Notice I said, "*we* often let it hold us back." *We*
are the ones who walk in the room troubled by our limp,
and *we* are the ones who convince ourselves that our limp
is a problem for others, so *we* are the ones who make
others concerned about our limp. But it doesn't have to
be this way!

Friends of ours had a beautiful black lab that was one
of the greatest dogs I've ever known. That boy, Jake,
was a beauty. One day Jake was found sitting by the
door unable to move his back legs; he had mysteriously
become paralyzed. The vet diagnosed a back injury, and
he operated on Jake and did the best he could. After six
months of rehab, that beautiful dog could walk again. He
didn't walk the way his friends did anymore; he had his
own way of slowly getting up and swinging one leg behind
the other. He even learned to run. He didn't run the way
his friends did, but he had his own way of getting up to
speed and running with his front legs while he hopped
with his back legs.

Our friends told us that sometimes when they had people
over, their guests would ask in a concerned voice, "Is your
dog okay?"

They'd smile and say, "He sure is!" Jake walked with a
limp, but he really didn't care. The other dogs in the

neighborhood didn't care, and neither did his owners. Jake went on to live another 10 years with his beautiful, unique limp.

We *all* walk with a limp, so it's time to stop worrying about what the person on the other side of the desk thinks about yours. One thing I can assure you: If your limp is not important to you, and you make peace with it, it will dramatically decrease the impact that your limp has on others. Too young, too old, too short, too tall, underqualified, overqualified, introverted, extroverted, physically or mentally challenged—it just doesn't matter.

The people you communicate with walk with their own limps, and they aren't concerned about your limp—they are concerned about your ability to walk with it.

Success requires humility, which is born of vulnerability.

Walk tall and make your limp part of the unique strengths you proudly offer the world. Once you embrace your shortcomings, they lose their hold over you and can no longer impede your success. Putting a lion in your heart has a lot to do with focus—a disciplined focus on good days *and* bad days.

Don't Be Afraid to Run in the Rain

Have you ever driven down a road on a cold and rainy Sunday and seen a miserable-looking runner chugging along? I'll bet you thought, *Why in the world would that knucklehead pick a day like today to run?* Well, I've been that runner, and there's a lot more to the picture than you might imagine. It involves an interesting form of disciplined behavior.

When I was younger, I loved to run. I started by running 10-kilometer races, then I graduated to 10-milers, moved on to half-marathons, and before I knew it I was running marathons. People would ask me, "What's it like to train for a marathon?"

I'd always have the same answer: "You have to be willing to do some running in the rain." I'd smile to myself because I knew most people had no idea what I was talking about. For me, *running in the rain* has always been a metaphor for something much greater.

To help you understand where I'm coming from, let me tell you how a person typically trains for a marathon. A race of 26.2 miles is not to be taken lightly. Most people cannot just show up and run a marathon, and yet almost anyone can complete one. How can that be? You just have to commit to training properly. That commitment involves nutrition and goal setting, but the most important aspect is the dedication to run a certain number of miles each week.

For instance, a typical amateur runner might commit to running 35 miles a week. That total is usually broken down into five runs, each representing a specific distance. No matter how many runs are planned or how long each one is, successful runners' weekly mileage totals are nonnegotiable. Depending on work commitments, family obligations, weather, and personal mood, some weeks are easier than others, but successful runners *never* miss getting in those miles each week.

Notice I emphasize the word *never.* That's because dedicated runners are suspicious and untrusting of the word *usually.* There are too many things that can affect something we "usually" do. We all can fall prey to the voices in our head that are masterful at providing a litany of excuses as to why we don't have to run that day—or that week. There can always be extenuating circumstances, which really mean that we just can't do our 35 miles that week.

I don't mean to imply that I didn't have my fair share of Sundays with a mileage count that was behind where it should have been, and some of those Sundays were rainy, but out I went. I had no one to blame but myself when I did. I was the knucklehead you saw running in the rain.

That philosophy has served me well in life and in business. When I wrote my first book in 1993, I had neither a mentor nor any experience tackling a project like that. What I did know was this: It represented a marathon of sorts, and I approached it in the same way. Instead of a weekly mileage count, I had a weekly page count.

This approach has served many others I work with, as well—including clients I mentor who are writing their own books. I have encouraged author-clients to set page-count goals and to never let their busy and challenging lives get in the way. All still have some unpleasant Sunday nights when they have no choice but to run in the rain. I ask for weekly page counts from authors, and I can see from the timestamps on their emails that many are up very late to write the promised pages. Of course many are either published authors or are well on their way to becoming published, and it is mostly because they allowed nothing to interfere with achieving their weekly page goals. Some would say these authors are lucky, but I see them following a disciplined process and making their own good luck.

When we hear the voices in our heads whining, *It's just not your week; you'll get 'em next week for sure*, breaking down the task into challenging but realistic nonnegotiable bites allows us to *never* falter. The voices don't disappear, but they fade to whispers when we stop listening.

You don't have to be training for a marathon or writing a book to benefit from this message. We all set goals; some are immediate, and some are long-term.

*It's the long-term goals
that require nonnegotiable
short-term commitments.*

Sometimes we may hit cold and rainy Sunday nights, but we still must lace up those shoes and run. It's all about discipline!

As you've probably noticed in this book, the world of getting others to believe in you and the world of dramatic acting frequently cross paths. A theater director named Cliff, whom I watched work with my kids, taught me a fundamental and invaluable approach to preparation that can have a big impact on the courage we all seek. It is excellent advice that pertains to the preparation for *any* high-pressure situation.

Locking It Down

The first time I watched Cliff work, I immediately liked him. He believed not only in the actors he worked with but also in their ability to experiment with their characters. His shows were legendary, but his success was by design, not coincidence.

Cliff was methodical in how he directed his shows. He would block a scene and direct the actors carefully and specifically. The actors would learn their lines and exactly where they needed to be onstage. Once he was satisfied that the cast had mastered the basics, he would turn them loose to explore their respective roles and performances.

He believed in the actors' ability to understand their characters, and he allowed them to make adjustments— up to a point. And therein lies the genius of this director.

▶ He knew that the initial changes the actors would make were based on a deeper understanding of their characters.

▶ He knew that the harder the actors worked to perfect their performance, the more risk they ran of becoming bored with it.

▶ He knew that once the actors became bored with the performance, they would be susceptible to confusing that boredom with inadequacy.

▶ He knew that the actors might become bored with the performance but that no audience, seeing it for the first time, would ever be.

As a result, Cliff had a rule that was strictly followed: Actors could experiment with a role until they were two weeks away from opening. Once they reached that two-week mark, they were told to "lock it down," which meant that under no circumstances were any further changes allowed. It was one of the secrets of his success as a director and a major reason why his productions were so powerful.

Repetition can be your best friend when preparing for any pressured situation, but it can also play tricks on your mind. Like an unwelcome friend, it can whine and nag its unsuspecting victim to listen to its voice of unreason: *If you just add a little here and change a little there, you can make it even better!* And therein lies the biggest mistake an actor can make when preparing for a show, a speaker can make when preparing a presentation, a writer can make when preparing a proposal, a job seeker can make when preparing a résumé—and anyone can make when preparing to earn the trust of another.

Never confuse what may feel stale to you with what appears to others as polish.

One can waste huge amounts of time constantly trying new things. What is really needed is the rehearsing of the same moves over and over until they become muscle memory. That in turn frees the mind to perform in the moment. Is there a greater gift for someone who must perform under pressure and is looking to be believed than the freedom to perform in the moment?

There are no exceptions to this rule, and no matter how appealing any new shiny object of change may appear, it should have no effect on you. That's because no matter how tempting that change may seem, you don't want to trade it for the confidence and the polish of the delivery you will experience by locking it down.

When you lock down what you are preparing, you give yourself the best chance to polish your words and your timing and perhaps most importantly increase your confidence. You might continue to daydream about your big meeting, but now your fantasies are not littered with the confusion of thinking about adding a little here or changing a little there.

There is a time for experimentation, and there's a time to lock it down. The next time you require a performance level of preparation, work your tail off to give yourself the best chance for success—then lock it down one week before go time. The results will be astonishing.

What Would You Attempt to Do?

Let's complete our brave goal of putting a lion in our heart by focusing on that amazing contraption that sits on top of our shoulders. The mind is remarkable—and it sure can fool you. Left unchecked it can convince you of all sorts of things. When the body is injured, the mind can convince you that you're just fine. When you hear something go bump in the night, the mind can convince you that there's trouble where there isn't. And when your spirit is low, sometimes the mind can convince you that this is where your spirit belongs.

Surely there have been times in your life when everything you touched seemed to work out for the better, and you sailed along without a care in the world. The mind was there for the ride, and it did its part, too. The mind gave you hope and optimism and told you to believe that whatever came next was going to follow the pattern of success you have enjoyed.

Of course, no life is without defeats, and sometimes those defeats bring about pain and worry. The mind was there to take that ride, too, and hope and optimism were replaced with doubt and pessimism. Worst of all, the mind convinced you to no longer believe in yourself.

Who says the mind is always right? Do we really have to wait around until life presents us with a string of successes to convince our minds to let us once again believe in ourselves?

We are far more believable to others when we believe in ourselves.

So, who says we can't *fool* the mind into believing?

Watch a method actor perform and you'll see what I mean. Method acting is a range of training and rehearsal techniques that actors use to encourage complete emotional identification with a character. For example, when an actor cries onstage and produces real tears, they are tapping into real emotion in their life by taking their mind to a moment in their past when they experienced that pain.

Much like a method actor, when we are struggling to believe in ourselves, we too can take our mind to another moment in time when we *did* believe. Whether it's meeting with a prospective employer or perhaps most importantly simply convincing others to believe us, tapping into the positive emotions associated with a past achievement can only increase our chances of success.

There is a quote by American pastor Robert H. Schuller that I keep in my office and look to for inspiration from time to time. It's a quote that my son, who is a professional comedian, has worn on a chain around his neck for years and one that I'd like *you* to keep with you, as well: *What would you attempt to do if you knew you could not fail?*

Forget your preoccupation with all the words you think are getting others to believe you. If you take your mind to a place you've been before when you *knew* you could not fail, the words will follow—but that's not all. Your mind will be happy to support those words with a more credible vocal pitch, pace, pause, and tone, as well as facial expressions and other nonverbal cues that ignite a passion in you that will be clearly visible to others.

We can't rid ourselves of fear and its effects on us, but we can certainly diminish their impact. Fear will not rule the day. It is merely a cluster of unknowns that are exacerbated by our imaginations. But knowledge is the enemy of fear, and when you put a lion in your heart, you can stand up to fear, and when you do, the victories will follow.

6

Positivity!

Let's turn our attention from how to get others to believe us to how to sustain that believability. I don't think it will surprise anyone to hear that carrying yourself in a positive way and displaying the traits of a positive person help—but there's one small problem: for some people thinking positively comes naturally; for others, well, let's just say they struggle with it.

What do *you* think: is positive thinking an innate behavior or can you be taught to think positively? It's an interesting question. The sticking point is not that some people are simply more positive than others; it goes deeper than that. So many people seem convinced that they would be more positive if there were something to be more positive *about*: "You either are or you aren't, and there isn't that much you can do about it!" I disagree. I believe that there is a basic formula to positivity and that it can in fact be taught.

I know many people struggle with positivity, but imagine if it *were* possible to learn a handful of basic guiding principles to living more positive lives. I believe that *anyone* can be happier and more optimistic, but they have to *want* it—no excuses, no reasons why it won't work; honestly *want* it!

To achieve positivity, we need to temporarily remove some major obstacles, beginning with health. Health is not fully within our control, so it can be eliminated as a core principle. What we eat, how we take care of our bodies, and how we manage stress are clearly contributing factors, but bad luck contributes, as well.

Next, we need to deal with money. I don't believe that money is tied to positivity, and I am not alone. You don't need to look any further than the fate of so many lottery winners; it rarely ends well. What's more, it's quite common for people to feel trapped by money, particularly when lifestyle costs slowly but surely creep up to keep pace with wealth. How many times have you heard someone older say, "We were never happier than when we were first starting out and had little money. We made do." You can't live without money, but it's no secret that money can cause problems, and in the long run it doesn't significantly affect our ability to be positive.

The third factor is genetics. In researching the subject, I found that there is significant debate among the medical community about the role that genetics plays in the pursuit of positivity. The debate centers not on whether genetics plays a part in our quest to be more positive but rather on what percentage of us are genetically limited in our ability to *be* positive. The numbers can vary, but clearly some of us struggle more than others. In some cases it is a genetic predisposition, and, like the issue of health, we can't change the genetic coding in our DNA. That leaves one last element: sheer luck.

Trust in Luck

I had a manager who once told me, "Jolles, luck is for losers!" I may have mistakenly believed it that day, but not now. Luck plays an important part in our lives, and, properly understood, not only can it improve our ability to remain positive but it can improve our odds of success. A foul ball that sailed 100 feet over my head at a baseball game reminded me of how true this is.

A few years ago, lightning struck in the second inning of a Washington Nationals game I was attending. Not real lightning—and my beloved Nats didn't pull off a triple play—but lightning by way of a screaming foul ball that flew over my head, crashed off the stadium wall, whistled back over another 50 rows of seats, and on the fly stuck like glue to my right hand—and I am left-handed!

There were 27,761 fans at the game, and I got to put a checkmark on my bucket list next to "Catch foul ball at baseball game." Pretty lucky, huh? It sure looked that way, but after a more careful examination, maybe it wasn't quite so lucky as you would think.

▶ Coincidently, when I was in fourth grade, I played a simple game of catch against my parent's brick bedroom wall. Without anyone to play catch with, I would toss a ball against that wall for hours on end. That little game took place almost daily for six years.

I sometimes still take a tennis ball outside and play a game of toss against the brick wall of my house. I guess you could say I am an expert at catching balls off walls.

▶ Coincidently, like every other left-handed person, I catch with my right hand. I guess you could say I caught a break, having that ball slicing toward my right.

▶ Coincidently, three years ago I had my only other chance of catching a foul ball not end up so well. Distracted and not paying attention as I rose to catch it, I made a small tactical error: I forgot to put down my aluminum beer bottle! I had instinctively raised it in the air like a baseball glove and watched helplessly as the ball landed on top of my bottle and ricocheted 20 rows behind me. (At least I didn't drop my beer!) I had never forgotten, however, how ill prepared I was at that moment, and I vowed to make sure that I would be ready if another chance ever presented itself. I guess you could say I learned from my mistake.

Do you see a pattern here? What looked like a serendip-itous situation wasn't quite as fluky as it appeared. Many obstacles that face us on a day-to-day basis may appear to be out of our control, yet there are steps we can take to increase our chances of success.

Practice It's no secret that the more we practice, the better we perform and the more positive we are heading into pressure situations. It was no coincidence that I had turned and was waiting for that ball to bounce off that wall while everyone else gave up after watching the ball sail over their heads. After years of practice, that move was instinctive.

Preparation I may not have brought my mitt that day, but I brought my instinct to catch with my right hand. My favorite brick wall and a couple of years of Little League Baseball had prepared me for that.

Focus I'd be lying if I didn't tell you how disappointed I was when I was caught unprepared with that beer in my hand. It is no coincidence that although I really am a fun guy at a ballgame, I'm also usually focused and aware of what's going on.

So, does practice, preparation, and focus guarantee you'll be successful in all your endeavors? Of course not. But it is fair to say that these actions can certainly increase your likelihood of success and enable you to approach in a positive way situations that are not in your control. In my case, I don't think the odds were anywhere near 27,761 to 1. I had significantly reduced those odds in my favor. Who knows when an odd moment of chance might come your

way. Assuming it's a meaningful moment, will you have
done the things you need to do to take advantage of it?

A willingness to invest in luck doesn't mean you will now
catch every foul ball that comes your way. You must still
be willing to stick out your hand and, although brave
in your attempt, risk losing. You must want something
to turn out in your favor and be willing to invest in it
mentally. That means if what you are feeling positive
about doesn't pan out, you need to look yourself in the
mirror—or your friends in the face—and say, "I was
hoping it would work out, but it didn't."

Allow Yourself to Hope

We underestimate hope. Hope gets us through tough
times. Although occasionally we may choose to give up on
it, hope will never desert us. Hope doesn't hold grudges. It
is only a thought away and is a powerful ally. Hope sounds
like the perfect companion; but if that's so, why are we so
quick to give up on hope? When I hear people say, "I don't
want to get my hopes up," it makes me wince. Why the
heck would you be afraid to get your hopes up?

*Positive people are
not afraid to hope.*

When was the last time you lessened your effort because you were hopeful? I've never heard of anyone who failed because they hoped too much. In fact, the opposite is true: When you have *real* hope, the chance of succeeding is not reduced—that's simply not possible. Hope generates energy. It produces resolve. It gives strength. It instills confidence. Hope can inspire you to do great things. So why do so few of us embrace hope, particularly when we seem to need it the most? What are we so afraid of?

It turns out there *is* a penalty for hope, and that is disappointment. When you get your hopes up and fail, disappointment is sure to follow. When this happens, we frequently lash out at hope. We blame our failure on hoping for something too much. Rather than attribute our failure to ourselves, we blame the concept of hope, saying, "If only I hadn't gotten my hopes up!"

Do you know what's worse than the sting of disappointment? The regret that comes with being too afraid to hope. That fear is frequently followed by being too afraid to try—and that is not an option.

Avoiding hope to prevent disappointment makes no sense, so throw caution to the wind. The next time you are pursuing something that isn't 100 percent under your control, give yourself a *double* dose of hope! If you don't succeed, don't attribute your disappointment to too much hope.

Graciously accept the disappointment that goes hand in hand with having high hopes.

Dust yourself off, try to learn from the experience, and get ready to hope some more! As a matter of fact, why not tell others about these challenges for which we hope so hard?

Let Others Know What You're Up To

Isn't it interesting how guarded we tend to be when it comes to letting others know about personal challenges that require courage? Fear of failure is a mighty foe, but letting others in on our tryst with failure requires even more courage. The risk is worth the reward.

Typically, when we plan to do something that requires courage, our instinct is to prepare for it but to tell absolutely no one about it. After all, the fear of the unknown is part and parcel of acts of courage. The more unknowns involved, the quieter we become. The more we can't control, the more private we are. The more vulnerable we feel as we face a big challenge, the less we want to talk about it. We don't always succeed at these acts of courage, but when we do we can't wait to tell others.

What if, rather than hide our acts of courage, we trumpeted our intentions to all in earshot?

This isn't just a hunch—it's an active tactic I use and coach others to use. I began trying this with authors I mentored. An author's instinct is to tell no one about their goal to write a book, to avoid awkward conversations from well-meaning friends who might ask how things are proceeding. By not telling anyone about their lofty goals, authors protect themselves from being confronted about a lack of progress.

It's another case of instinct versus logic. When you tell others that you are working on a book, it's an uncomfortable topic, particularly when you've never written a book before. It's only natural for people to ask you about it. When an author is trying to develop a book, however, one of the greatest gifts they can be given is to be asked about it. The questions help them prepare and practice for more important scenarios that require articulate and succinct responses. But that's not all. When a writer is working on a concept, the more they talk about it, the more ideas come from those conversations. Where do you think many of my BLArticle ideas come from?

This same philosophy is true for all kinds of challenges. When you tell others you are in a career transition, it's an uneasy topic, but it's natural for people to ask you about it. It takes courage to put yourself out there and ask for help. Not talking about it might be instinctive, but it certainly isn't logical. Why would anyone want to keep a job search a secret? When you let others know, you extend your network. A recent survey by The Adler Group places the number of job hirings as a result of a network connection at a staggering 85 percent!

Do you see a pattern here? The downside of telling others about goals that truly require courage is our fear of failure to achieve those goals. Personally, I respect those who try and fail!

The upside? When others know of our goals:

▶ We tend to work harder to achieve them.

▶ We tend to expand our network of ideas.

▶ We tend to stay committed to those goals.

I think the upside here far outweighs the downside. That's why I'm a big fan of putting our courageous challenges in the public eye for all to see. Whether you're writing a book, transitioning jobs, running a marathon, climbing a mountain, or taking steps to begin your journey to establishing a new level of credibility, it requires courage. Let 'em hear you!

Act Positively

How many times have you received a phone call or
been asked by someone, "How are you doing?" You are
probably asked that question every day, often multiple
times. I've heard all kinds of answers to that rather
trite question:

- ▶ "Hanging in there." That's from people who want
  you to know that they are struggling.

- ▶ "Okay." That's from people who prefer you don't ask
  the question.

- ▶ "Same old, same old" or "I can't complain." That's
  from people who are too lazy to even attempt to
  answer the question.

When I am asked this question, I have a rather unusual
way of answering it; it typically catches people by surprise,
and it usually makes them smile. For more than 40 years,
my answer has always been the same: "I'm happy."

Am I *always* happy when I give that answer? I'll never tell,
but I will admit that one reason why I answer that way is
to remind myself to be positive!

Often when I give that reply, I hear the follow-up
question: "Well, what's *making* you happy?!" Frequently,
I don't have the answer front of mind because I've trained
myself to respond the way I do. I will always answer,
however, by forcing myself on the spot to think of

something that's making me happy. This exercise helps me look for the good things in life and remain positive.

Can acting positively make you more positive? Absolutely!

There have been experiments in which subjects have been asked to smile. As they are told to turn up the corners of their mouths, sensors indicate that they do indeed feel more positive when they put on a happy face.

Should *you* change how you answer the question *How are you doing?* Not necessarily, but going through the motions can trigger the emotion. You just need to remind yourself of the blessings in your life and to remain positive. Is that such a tough job? Well, it can be when you confront the antithesis of positivity: worry.

Banish the Word *Worry*

I've never been a fan of the word *worry*. (I'm not fond of the word *nervous* either.) Of course, like everyone else, I have been apprehensive from time to time, but I just don't like that word. I hear the word *worried*, and I think of someone sitting in a corner, chewing their nails and hoping for a solution over which they seem to have no control.

As an athlete, I never wanted to play a game when I was in a worried state of mind. As a coach, I never wanted to mentor a team who were worried. As a salesman, I never wanted to meet with a client while I was worried. As a speaker, I never take the stage worried. Even *Merriam-Webster's Collegiate Dictionary* doesn't seem fond of the word, defining *worry* as "to assail with rough or aggressive attack or treatment; torment" and "to feel or experience concern or anxiety; fret."

How in the world can worry contribute to one's success? Years ago I banished the word from my vocabulary; and if there were a way to create a junk word list in my Microsoft Word program, *worry* would be the first one in it. You won't hear that word come out of my mouth. Of course, I had to find a replacement, so I chose the word *anxious*. *Merriam-Webster* seems more comfortable with this word, too: "ardently or earnestly wishing."

This may sound like semantics to you, but it goes deeper than that. I've never known anyone to become more believable when they are worried. When my kids used to tell me they were worried about something, I would tell them, "If I thought worrying about it would improve my chances of success by even 1 percent, I would be one of the most spectacular, competitive worriers you ever saw!"

As for being anxious, *that* I can relate to. You can channel that anxiousness to energy and focus to contribute to your success. It's amazing sometimes what a simple word change can do for your outlook. Rather than push the thought of worry away, you can embrace the idea of being eager to tackle what's ahead—with hope and focus.

One of my favorite quotes by author Dan Zadra, which sits by my coffee maker so that I can see it when I start my day, says it best: "Worry is a misuse of the imagination."

Are you guilty of misusing your imagination from time to time? Ban that worry and replace it with a more productive use of your mind.

Keep Things in Perspective

It happens all the time in sports: One team is playing well, coasting along, and everything they do seems to be working. Then in the blink of an eye, the momentum changes. Everything that was effortless becomes strained. The harder the team works to recover, the more unnatural their efforts become. Panic sets in, and before you know it the tables have turned.

I've coached a lot of basketball games, and I've often seen this scenario play out. It isn't due to bad luck or poor decision-making. Games in sports are often decided by momentum, and it's not uncommon for the team that is trailing to use their desperation to dig deeper: The players get a burst of adrenaline and they shift into a higher gear. Before you know it, the team that is leading panics, losing both their focus and the game.

I would call a time-out when I saw my team's lead begin to slip. For more than 30 years, I always began my pep talk in the same way. As the players gathered around with fear in their eyes, I'd look at the scoreboard, smile, and make note of how many points we were leading by. Maybe our lead had shrunk from 15 to 5. Whatever the number was, I'd start the conversation with our lead. For example, if my team were ahead by only two points, I'd say this:

I'd rather be up by two than down by two.

It's not rocket science, but I saw firsthand what that statement did to the players' psyches. Putting the situation in perspective helped the team regroup and refocus. This approach was effective not just for teams that were losing their lead; it also helped teams that were trailing: After all, I'd rather be trailing by six than trailing by 12.

Life throws curveballs at all of us, and it has momentum shifts, as well. Perhaps these scenarios will resonate:

▶ Your business has been suffering some setbacks, and your prospect list is down to a handful of clients.

▶ Your cash flow has dwindled to 50 percent of its past volume.

Wouldn't it be helpful in each of these situations to remind yourself of the bigger picture?

▶ I'd rather have a handful of clients to call on and build from than no clients at all.

▶ I'd rather have 50 percent of my recent cash flow than 25 percent.

Looking at the bigger picture doesn't alleviate the pain of challenging situations, but it sure helps put things in perspective. Momentum can be a fickle friend, and no one is impervious to occasional momentum shifts. Successful people tend to look at the bright side of challenging situations. Once again, by training your mind with phrases like, *I'd rather be* _____ *than* _____, you teach yourself how to stay positive.

Believe in You—Not Jinxes!

I believe that the most illogical aspect of positivity is the near superstitious effects it can have on people. Just the mention of positivity makes some people cringe. But I'm a superstitious guy. I won't eat certain foods on certain days. I won't hit a snooze bar. I have a lucky tie and cufflinks and small silver lighting bolt I wear when I step on a stage in front of an audience. I try to find logical reasons for my little superstitions, but the truth is I do some of these things because I don't want to somehow jinx myself. And believe me: I understand jinxes.

There's one jinx I don't buy into, however, and that's the bizarre superstition of being afraid to believe in yourself. We think we will somehow jinx ourselves if we express positive thoughts about ourselves publicly. Don't believe me? How many times have you heard an exchange similar to this?

> Person A: "Do you think you'll achieve that goal?"

> Person B: "I don't know. I've worked really hard, but I'd hate to say yes and jinx myself."

Since when did believing in yourself become a jinx?! Why not have the audacity to utter those positives out loud? Will a jinx fairy come down from the sky and smite us with bad luck dust? I think not. In fact, I believe that the opposite is true.

Listen to the tone and words of people who confidently speak about things that are not 100 percent in their control. Not only will you believe them but you'll see that they believe in themselves. Assuming you've worked hard and done what's necessary to be successful, why wouldn't you allow others to hear you speak about yourself positively?

What are we so afraid of? Maybe we don't want to be perceived as arrogant. Really? I don't believe that telling others that we are confident that our efforts will result in a positive outcome will make them think we are bragging or arrogant.

Confidence is not conceit.

Perhaps it's the fear of failure. After all, if we don't tell people that we expect to be successful and instead keep our hopeful expectations a secret, a possible failure won't be so traumatic. I have a lot more respect for people who put themselves out there with their goals on the line than those who sound timid or unsure for fear that they will jinx their chances of success.

It boils down to instinct versus logic. Instinctively, many coaches—particularly new ones—tend to avoid laying out large goals for their teams. These coaches will tell you that they don't want to put unnecessary pressure on their players and then see disappointment if they don't achieve the goals. More-skilled coaches are upfront with such goals. They make sure their players believe in the goals, too. There is no logic to believing that talking about goals will jinx your efforts. In fact, the complete opposite is true: goals motivate people to work harder and with more enthusiasm. In telling others about your goals, you establish a support system that holds you accountable—and makes you work even harder.

Having the courage to speak positively about things that are not completely under your control does not manifest some mythical jinx! Let's stop whispering about our hopes and dreams and instead shout them from the rooftops! Win, lose, or draw, if we've put in the work to achieve our goals, we can be proud of our effort regardless of the outcome.

Take Stock of What You Have

We all at times take stock of what we have—what is
working for us—and we should celebrate those moments.
I'd like to share a story about a mishap on one of my many
road trips. This misfortune is significant because it taught
me a key lesson that I hope will ring true to you.

The sad part of the story goes like this: Rob finishes his
seminar in New York. Rob meets up with his family. Rob
and family take the Long Island Railroad to Long Beach to
spend a few days with their wonderful friends the Grazis.
Rob helps family with their luggage and upon exiting the
train finds that his laptop bag—containing, among other
things, his un-backed-up computer with 90 percent of
a manuscript representing five years of work on its hard
drive, keys, cords, books, sunglasses, credit cards, and
more—is missing. In more than three decades of hefty
travel, Rob has never had a lost bag, let alone one that he
kept in his possession. Rob is devastated—but that's not
the story.

The happy part of the story goes like this: Thirty minutes
after departing the train, while being consoled by his
friend and waiting to file a police report, Rob's phone
rings. It turns out someone had seen the unattended
laptop bag and decided to "protect" it, removing it from
the train and taking it home. Twenty minutes later Rob
and his laptop bag are reunited. Rob is elated—but that's
not the story, either.

Rob wasn't just happy; Rob was jubilant. As a matter of fact, Rob was happier than Rob had been for quite some time. Wasn't having finished a successful seminar enough to make him happy? After all, Rob was finishing his best month of consulting in a year and a half without any real celebration or fanfare.

Wasn't meeting up with his wife and daughter for a nice trip enough to make him happy? Spending time away with your loved ones usually puts a smile on most people's faces, including Rob's, and yet Rob was almost going through the motions of affection for them both.

Wasn't visiting two of his closest friends in their beautiful waterfront home enough? Rob and his wife have seen the Grazis at least a couple of times a year for more than 30 years, and they always have a nice time, and yet Rob was focused on the long train ride to see them. It was a 45-minute train ride.

Rob had all of these wonderful blessings in his life, and yet having his laptop bag go missing and then be found is what it took to make him truly happy. Staring catastrophe in the face—and then averting it—is what it took. And *that* is the story.

Why is it that we take for granted the very things we should rejoice in and are not truly happy until something lost is returned? How often do we take stock of our good health only *after* a health scare? How often do we thank our lucky stars for the job we have only *after* our name does not appear on a list of layoffs?

I was ecstatic to have been reunited with my laptop bag—and I stayed that way! I went to bed happy, woke up happy, wandered around the entire day happy, had dinner happy, went back to bed happy, woke up again, and reveled in the sheer joy of my many blessings. Why do we recognize what we have only when threatened with losing it? Why is it so hard to live on the positive side of life and maintain a happy outlook?

When it comes to being a positive person, don't believe that you either are or you aren't. Positivity can be learned. Just follow the basic formula to effect positive change in your life: trust in luck; practice, prepare, and focus; allow yourself to hope; act positively; banish the word *worry*; keep things in perspective; believe in yourself and not jinxes; and appreciate what you have.

7

The Politics of Success

The topic of office politics seems to live in dark corners that most acknowledge but few want to talk about. We know it exists; we just choose not to discuss it in schools and even at home with our children. Ignoring it won't make it go away, and the repercussions of not being politically astute can derail anyone's career, personal journey, and self-esteem. Why can't we just write down the political pitfalls in the workplace, write solutions to address them, and have employees study the manual? Doesn't that beat the alternative?

The fact is, many good-natured people assume that they can manage their way through the political minefield. This is a real-world issue, and many well-meaning people struggle to cope with the reality of politics when working with others. Achieving believability is a tremendous accomplishment—but sustaining it as we maneuver through the quagmire of personal politics can be a real challenge.

Lest you think that negotiating people politics has been easy for me, in the interest of full disclosure it has certainly not. There is a phrase that I once used in every political conversation I found myself in, typically when someone was trying to help me. I would repeat it over and over. It took me 10 years to stop saying it, but I can remember it clearly: "Someday they're going to put on my tombstone, *This guy never gave in to office politics and always stayed true to his beliefs.*"

Isn't that lovely? So noble and heartfelt—and so utterly misguided. Whenever you hear someone make a statement like that, what they're really saying is, "I don't want to be part of the politics of people regardless of the outcome." At first blush that might sound diplomatic, but is it sensible?

Let's define *office politics* and see if that helps us. Finding a definition was more difficult than I thought. *Merriam-Webster's* definitions of *playing politics* include "to say or do things for political reasons instead of doing what is right or what is best for other people" and "political activities characterized by artful and often dishonest practices."

Well, at least now we know why most of us struggle mightily with the subject! We are trained to believe that all office politics are detrimental and cultivated by devious people. Further, it seems like those with the audacity to recognize and participate in office politics must have somehow sold their souls. But those are not the only interpretations out there. I like one of wiseGEEK's definitions: "Office politics is simply the playing out of interrelationships within office environments."

Often people blur the lines between the terms *politics* and *principles*. I suppose it's easy to confuse the two, particularly for those who deplore office politics. *Merriam-Webster* defines *principle* as "a moral rule or belief that helps you know what is right and wrong and that influences your actions."

Can we agree that the "playing out of interrelationships in an office environment" does not have to include putting ourselves in conflict with the standards we set for our personal conduct? Rather than keep our heads down in the hope that office politics will not creep into our mental cubicle, I suggest that it's wiser to prepare for the inevitable. That doesn't mean selling out or being gossipy or manipulative, but rather preparing ourselves so that we can avoid the pain of being on the wrong side of interpersonal relationships.

The typical way that employees rise to management positions has little to do with interpersonal skills but rather, sadly, with how proficient they are at their job. Fortunately, with no experience and no management skills, at least *new* managers are typically provided training. Oops, my mistake: most in management or positions of authority are given zero training on basic management skills and how to work well with others. So, if a difficult boss is more the norm, let's figure out how to prepare for this scenario.

Step In and Manage the Difficult Boss

An effective boss can communicate clearly and manage fairly, and there is a clear understanding that the more successful you become, the more successful your boss can become.

That might sound simplistic, but that simple concept of management is usually the litmus test for what makes a good manager. Some "get it" and some don't. To learn how to manage a difficult boss, you first have to learn how to manage those who *don't* "get it."

It's sad to catch the hurt in a person's voice when they say something like, "I don't understand what I did wrong. My boss just doesn't like me." It's like seeing someone's pained reaction to hearing that there is no Santa Claus. Realizing that your boss is not effective can be depressing. So, how do you manage an ineffective boss? Let's dissect the above litmus test and examine these management principles individually.

▶ *"An effective boss can communicate clearly..."* If your manager doesn't do this, you're going to have to do it for them. Speak up when you don't understand an assignment. Cover your tracks with an email or document confirming what is being asked of you. Go the extra mile to ensure that you and your boss do communicate clearly.

▶ *"and manage fairly..."* One of the disappointing repercussions of working for a manager who doesn't manage fairly is the ripple effect it can have on team morale. There can be dissension and resentment toward the manager and toward one another. It's easy to get caught up in a negative free-for-all, but that can result in serious issues for you personally. Even if the boss doesn't manage the team fairly, it doesn't mean that *you* can't be fair in your dealings

with your colleagues. Take the high road and stay
out of the fray.

▶ *"and there is a clear understanding that the more
successful you become, the more successful your boss
can become."* This is the big one. When a boss understands this, they work to help you succeed, and you
will do all you can to help the boss succeed. When a
boss *doesn't* understand this, however, they see your
success as a problem for them. It's not that your boss
doesn't like you—it's that the boss is concerned that
you are going to outshine them and possibly gun for
their job. To combat this effectively, you need to be
outspoken about how *your* success is a result of *their*
support. You will be much better off in your boss's
eyes if you make it clear that you do not see your
personal intentions as intersecting with your boss's
personal intentions.

The moral of the story is this: Having a great boss is often
an exception rather than the rule, and a good boss takes
little or no management. When you find yourself with
a boss who truly cares about your well-being, consider
it a blessing and not a moral obligation that is owed to
you. If, on the other hand, you find yourself with a boss
who sees your success as a threat—one who just doesn't
get it—it's up to *you* to think like a good boss. Managers
don't usually wake up and think, *I feel like being a lousy
boss today*—they just don't understand what it takes to be
a *good* boss. You do—so manage your boss accordingly;

you will not only be helping yourself but you'll be helping your boss as well!

Now that you have a better understanding of how to deal with a difficult boss, be careful not to jump to conclusions. Sometimes a manager might just be nervous, having a bad day, or perhaps dealing with something outside the organization that is causing them pain—just like you do from time to time. Be careful not to misread any person you work with because sometimes your first impression may be way off base. Don't assume you know what others are thinking, and don't infer other people's intentions.

Beware of Misreads

You know what really gets to me? People who don't make eye contact. You know what that means: they don't have time for you. In fact, it seems like some people go out of their way to avoid eye contact. And you know what that means: they don't care about you. Oh, and how about when these people often don't even smile. You know what that means: they don't even like you.

We've seen and reacted to such people for years. When we were in school, we'd see them on a regular basis. We've seen them at the office, at the health club, in the store, in the neighborhood, or just about anywhere. Their failure to do something as simple as making eye contact or smiling makes us wonder. Before we know it, we begin to misuse our imagination.

▶ Is he too busy to even nod hello? Jerk!

▶ Did he actually look down rather than look at me as I walked by? How dare he!

▶ Is he so much better than me that he can't even smile at me? Knucklehead!

At first, it doesn't really bother us that much. I mean, they could simply be busy, distracted, or preoccupied. But if after a while we notice a pattern of avoidance, it can be infuriating. We begin to retaliate, firing back with our *own* lack of eye contact. When we see them coming, our mood changes. Like a pitcher winding up for a fastball, we throw our best dismissive look right back at them as if to say, *How do you like **them** apples!*

Does this sound familiar? It hurts to be ignored or dismissed by others. You wonder: *Is this lack of civility because I'm not important enough, or attractive enough, or cool enough, or interesting enough? I mean, for goodness' sake, how hard can it be to just **acknowledge** someone! The nerve of these people!*

But what if we have it all wrong?

What if their lack of eye contact *isn't* because we're considered worthless or unattractive or of no social value? What if it has nothing to do with us at all? What if it's a complete misread of the other person? What if such people who commit this social crime are just…*shy*?

I once coached a client who told me that he watched a guy stare at the floor and frown every time he got near him—for more than a *decade*. After a couple of years, goaded by his fragile ego, my client threw it right back at the guy. He grew accustomed to their little grudge match of disinterest and face-making until one day the guy came up to him, stared at the floor, and told him what a good job he had done on a project. As a matter of fact, while frowning at my client, the guy offered his hand to shake! My client said than when he shook the guy's hand he noticed something else: this person who he was convinced disliked him was wrestling with a smile. He also noticed that he instantly *liked* the guy—and they've been friends ever since.

Often the seeming uncivil act of not making eye contact could simply be insecurity. Not everyone is a social butterfly. The next time you smile at someone but they look away, try not to take it personally; say "hi" anyway. I would bet that you will be surprised by both the sincere "hello" you hear and the look of gratitude that you are given.

Know When—and How—to Be Right

Thinking you are right is a blind spot, not just for intellectuals but for anyone who places being right above being sensitive to their surroundings. Allowing others to be right, even when you believe there is a better way, is not a weakness; rather, it displays strength of character. It's not about being right; it's about *when* to be right.

Being right can come at a cost, and it's amazing how many business schools skip this basic fact. While taking my business classes at the University of Maryland, I learned the principles of economics, accounting, statistics, and so much more. One thing I was *not* taught was about the real-world politics of business. Without a teacher, I was left to my own instincts—and those of my father.

My father's instincts served him well as a Marine and they served him well as a salesman. He never really had to deal with corporate politics because he was a damn good salesman. When you work for an organization that is driven by sales and you outsell those around you, as he did, there are no politics.

Being mentored by my father, I took pride in being known as a guy who would not be silent when he knew he was right. At Xerox I welcomed the price for being right because I knew the courage it took to do so. I battled management and my coworkers when I knew I was right. I dare to admit that a part of me, deep down, enjoyed those battles. I wore my beliefs like a badge of honor that I displayed with enormous satisfaction. I even threw in my patented *They're going to put it on my tombstone* mantra from time to time. I was wrong.

There's a time, a place, and a way to be right.

Xerox Corporation put up with me because I worked hard and consistently exceeded expectations, but the truth is I was operating under an uneasy truce with those around me. I became disenchanted with the tension that being right seemed to create in others, so I left to become an entrepreneur.

I could give a number of reasons why I left Xerox, but the truth is I left so that I could be right. I wasn't courageous, and I wasn't right. I was lucky. If I could jump into the Wayback Machine and sit down with a young, starry-eyed Rob Jolles who was hell-bent on being right, I'd tell him a few things that he needed to hear.

▶ I'd tell him not to confuse the courage to stand up for your beliefs with the proper time and place to take that stand.

▶ I'd tell him not to confuse the pride of ownership of an idea or belief with the importance of being a contributing team player who can support the ideas of others.

▶ I'd tell him not to confuse supporting the second-best idea with selling out.

▶ I'd tell him to stop focusing on what's written on his
tombstone and instead learn to focus on having the
courage to be wrong sometimes.

When you work for a company and are part of a team, you
want to be a team player. You want them to know that you
can support the ideas of others and that you understand
that there is a time and a place and a way to be right. This
is rarely taught in business school, and there is still no
Wayback Machine. If in the past you alienated others with
your need to be right, you can now work in the present to
ensure that being right is not at the cost of being an asset
to a company and a team.

Learn How to Disagree

It always amazes me how misunderstood the simple act
of disagreeing can be. We all know that disagreeing is a
healthy part of any relationship, whether it's business or
personal. Mahatma Gandhi once said, "Honest disagreement is often a good sign of progress." Avoiding disagreement is simply not an option.

One of the reasons why disagreement fails is because
it's trickier than it appears, and we are rarely, if ever,
taught how to disagree constructively. We are left with a
paradox: without disagreement we cannot progress, and
with it we potentially place ourselves in danger. So, let's
tease this out by looking at four general areas to focus

on when disagreeing: the words, the sound, the face, and the timing.

The words Words really matter here. In a corporate environment, it's often difficult to raise your hand and simply disagree. It's healthy, but it's an exceptional group that gets along so well that no one cares if you disagree in public. That doesn't mean we can't disagree in front of a team, but it does mean we have to find some better words. I've always been a fan of what I call a *support/build*—a process that supports one person's idea while clearing the way for disagreement by allowing others to build on it. It sounds something like this:

> PERSON A: I propose that we start charging for internal project support.

> PERSON B: I think finding a revenue source is an excellent idea *[support]*. How about we look at all the available avenues to make sure we can generate revenue and retain the support we need from our other departments *[build]*.

The sound There's nothing worse than hearing someone disagree with well-thought-out words that just don't sound genuine. Using words that aren't "in tune" is a missed opportunity that can sow distrust. As discussed in earlier chapters, I firmly believe that we are quite capable of having the sounds we are making line up with the words we are using. The truth is, we often want the other person to question whether our response is sincere. When you truly believe what you are saying, your tune will sound just fine and you are more likely to be believed by others.

The face It's been well established that your facial expressions convey more of the emotion behind your message than your words, tune, or other nonverbal cues. Whether it works for or against you, your face is a window to your sincerity. Much like getting our words and tune in sync, our words should line up with our facial expressions as well. That fake smile—or as my Egyptian friends would call it, that "yellow" smile—isn't fooling anyone. Unless you want a confrontation, reach peace with whatever is bothering you, and your face will not betray your words.

The timing There are colleagues, often in positions of power, who couldn't care less what you have to say if it isn't said at the right time. There is a time and a place to disagree, and knowing when the timing is right is a definite strength. Who really thinks that taking on a dominant manager in front of the team, or friend in front of your peers, is appropriate timing and gives you the best chance for success?

It's never too late to learn how and when to disagree— and how you disagree can mean the difference between a constructive relationship and one fraught with dysfunction.

Heed Your Own Advice

A few years ago, I had lunch with a man named Ron, the first manager I ever worked for. I had worked for him more than 30 years ago, and although I did not realize it at the time, he was probably the best manager I ever had. He taught me how to sell, how to manage my time, and so much more. What made our reunion so amazing was that this time he taught me a simple lesson he had recently taught himself—and he believes that it saved his life.

Ron was not your average, run-of-the-mill manager. He ran an insurance office that comprised more than 100 people, including some 70 salespeople, support staff, assistant managers, trainers, and administrators. He helped make the office, located in Washington, DC, one of the most successful in the country. If you ask him, he'll tell you his best work was with the sales team.

Selling insurance can be a brutal profession, with a washout rate that's quite sobering. It takes a special person to be able to listen, problem-solve, instill confidence, show empathy, and care. But, as he put it, the most difficult task was to look a person in the eye and tell them, "You need to pull yourself up by your bootstraps, dust yourself off, and fight!"

This wasn't the first time I'd reconnected with Ron. In fact, I've met with him nearly annually for the past 10 years. Each time I saw him, he looked a little worse for wear than the previous time. He's had a few personal setbacks, including enduring the sorrow of losing his wife—the love of his life. The last time I had seen him he had looked despondent and distant, and I sadly wondered if that was going to be the last time. But at this most recent lunch, Ron looked *much* better. As he walked in, he was smiling and confident, and he was teasing me about my bald head. He was back!

Well into his eighties, Ron spoke about the presentations he was delivering and the volunteer counseling he was doing at his assisted-living facility for those who were battling depression. After about 15 minutes of listening to how he not only came back from the brink but was now helping others, I asked him point-blank: "What happened to you? You look like a completely different person from the man I saw last year."

His answer was simple: "Rob, for over 40 years I've managed people who struggled at home and on the job, and I always found the words to help them. Sometimes those words were motivational and sometimes they were tough, but they were always honest. In short, I decided to sit myself down and have a frank conversation with myself. I asked myself, *What would I tell myself if I were still a manager?* I found the words I would tell others in my situation, and at that exact moment, everything became clearer and easier to understand."

The solution here may sound simplistic, but I saw his transformation with my own eyes. Isn't it interesting how often the answers we seek are right there in front of us? If you are struggling, ask yourself: *If I were helping someone else with this issue, what would I tell them?* I often take the question to a personal level by asking myself, *If my son or daughter asked me about the issue I am struggling with, how would I advise them?* When you ask these questions in this way, you'll be astounded at the clarity of your response.

Double Your Efforts to Address Your Weaknesses

I've coached a bunch of basketball players, but one of my favorites was a young man named Ryan. Not blessed with great height, he fell in love with the position of point guard, which allowed him to relay my plays and manage the flow of the game. It was the perfect position for Ryan, who liked to lead and control things.

Being left-handed gave him an initial advantage over his opponents. Because most defenders assumed he was right-handed and most likely moving to his right, he had the element of surprise on his side. It's not unusual for coaches and players to study their opponents during warm-ups. Knowing this, he developed his own sneaky way of warming up.

Although Ryan was uncomfortable dribbling or moving to his right, he'd warm up almost exclusively using his right hand. Once the game began, he would dribble the ball up court with his right hand, and as soon as he got near the top of the key he would cross over to his left. This always left his defender flatfooted. From there Ryan would drive to the basket for an easy layup. This little trick never failed to work the first time, and with his defender thinking it was an anomaly, it would often work the second time, too.

But by the third time, his defender would be waiting for him. The element of surprise had been replaced by predictability. Going to his left was easy and natural to Ryan, but he knew what he had to do to become a much better player. He had to put in the time and the effort to learn how to use his right hand, or what basketball players call the *off-hand*.

In baseball this off-hand is the difference between learning to hit a fastball and learning to hit a curveball. In tennis it's the difference between learning to hit a flat serve and learning to hit a kick serve. In golf it's the difference between learning to hit a golf ball and learning to spin a golf ball. If you want to perform like an amateur, or only be successful against amateurs, you don't have to worry about any of this. But against more-skilled competition, without putting the time into these elements, you'll get crushed.

We often operate in one of two areas in our lives. One area is that place where everything feels natural and effortless. This area makes us feel confident, and here we are often celebrated for our expertise and accomplishments. This is the area that makes us good at what we do.

The other area represents our off-hand. It's the part of our job that does not feel natural and requires effort. We don't feel confident, and we avoid having to use our off-hand skills. When we avoid what doesn't come naturally, our off-hand becomes weaker. What's more, when we avoid using our off-hand, we make it obvious to others just where our strengths and weaknesses lie. You would think that seeing someone excel at a skill would put them in a position of strength, but I feel it does the opposite: it makes us one-dimensional and vulnerable. Vulnerable to what? Change.

Don't be typecast. When an actor is celebrated for incredible, focused portrayals of a certain type of character, they are described by a word that makes them shudder: *typecast.* If there is a role that matches directly with their celebrated strength, they are hired. But track the lives of some of your favorite actors who were typecast early in their careers, and the very strength that brought them success eventually becomes their downfall. The smart ones took roles early on that played against their stereotype, and they not only survived but broadened

their repertoires. The ones who never developed their
off-hand characters faded into obscurity.

Shine in the light of your natural and celebrated skills while working on your off-hand.

US management guru Jim Collins opens his best-seller
Good to Great by saying, "Good is the enemy of great."
If you want to be great, identify your off-hand and work
twice as hard to develop it. Be prepared not only to be
frustrated but also to fight off the voices in your head that
will tempt you to take the easier route and focus on what
comes naturally. If writing is a weakness, enroll in an
adult education program. If you avoid public speaking at
all costs, join Toastmasters. If you hate selling, read one
of my books and give me a call! Expanding your comfort
zone by developing your off-hand skills will have them
coming naturally to you in no time.

It's the Little Pieces That Count the Most

When was the last time you began a large project but ran
out of steam before finishing it? You're in good company,
but that doesn't mean you're off the hook. My dad used
to love to work on model tanks (of all things), and he
was darn good at it. He would spend hours working on a

model, meticulously assembling every piece, then every decal, then finishing the job with his own camouflage paint combinations. He would put his finished products in my room, and I admired them so much that I decided to try building one myself.

Dad took me to the hobby store, and after much discussion I decided that my first model would be a car. As soon as we got home, I eagerly opened the box and was greeted by sheets of connected plastic pieces, followed by a sheet of decals. The instructions were a little intimidating, but I couldn't wait to get started.

The beginning was a lot of fun. The endeavor was new, and the first moves were easy. Between the excitement of starting and the large initial pieces I was snapping together, I immediately dubbed myself an expert model builder. Within 20 minutes, my model surprisingly resembled the car on the box I had propped up next to my workstation!

But then the project slowed down, the pieces got smaller, and it became increasingly more challenging to work with the small parts that were the final touches. Finishing the project wasn't nearly as fun as starting it, and it required discipline I hadn't yet acquired. My momentum was gone, I lost interest, and the remaining pieces lay scattered on the rug. I put my green plastic car—minus the details, decals, and paint—next to my dad's beautiful tanks.

It was a painful testament to my inability to finish what
I had started.

Does this sound familiar? No one enters a challenging
scenario with the plan to quit, but many challenging tasks
follow a similar pattern. The initial steps are fun, easy, and
exciting and fill us with hope; but it's the final little pieces
that truly challenge us and take us to the next level.

The finishing touches are what transform our projects from good to great.

It's the little pieces that teach us that we must remain
diligent and disciplined to complete a task. The big pieces
bring us hope, but it's the little pieces that bring the
project to fruition.

As the proverb goes, *forewarned is forearmed*: prior
knowledge of possible problems gives one a tactical
advantage. By reminding yourself not to lose steam
before the finishing touches of a larger project, you
can prepare to head off that eventuality. Pace and time
management are common, often unconscious, behaviors,
so your mindfulness is key. That means understanding
that the small pieces—the ones that take more time,
concentration, and discipline to complete—may very well

define who you are. Prepare for them, plan for the time and effort required to address them properly, and finish them—because it's the little pieces that count the most.

Moving Past a Breakup

Coaching and mentoring will not spare you from one of life's most personally damaging events: a breakup. Being told that we are no longer wanted in business or in love has the potential to devastate even the strongest and most confident individuals. It can generate a negative energy that can crush the human spirt and follow us wherever we go. Much like the end of a marriage, sometimes breakups are easy and sometimes they're not; and every now and then, they are downright cruel.

Experiencing cruelty can be heartbreaking and, even worse, leave us bitter and confused. When we have been asked to leave, and feel that we have been treated unfairly, it is crushing and painful. Such breakups often occur in intense, dysfunctional relationships, and it's not easy to move on from something like that.

The worst part of all is what happens next: we carry that confusion, pain, and anger with us, and before long it infects our spirit; it makes us cynical and impedes our happiness. Even if you haven't lived through this experience, you probably know someone who has. When someone is coping after a breakup, any conversation you have with them will eventually allude to the sadness and darkness they are feeling. One story leads to another, and each one taps a deeper level of pain and rage.

Part of the scars we bear are self-inflicted due to our inability to move past the pain. That emotional baggage can lead to a free-fall of despair and depression and prevents us from moving on. I can tell you confidently that there *is* a way out. Complete the following process, and you will be free to get on with your life and move forward to the next place you are meant to be.

Begin with self-reflection. Start by asking yourself this question: *If I had a do-over, what could I have done differently?* Yes, you have been wronged and, yes, you have a right to be angry, but no matter how you spin it, no scenario places the full blame of a breakup squarely on only one party's shoulders. There is a lesson to be learned, and if you learn it, not only will you move toward healing but you'll be rewarded by never making that mistake again.

Accept the 90-10 principle. It is not unusual for people who have gone through a breakup to struggle with accepting any blame whatsoever. That's where the 90-10 principle comes in with a new question: *Assuming that you are 90 percent without fault, what would be the 10 percent for which you can take responsibility?*

When you answer this question honestly, you will transform your misery into an opportunity to evolve and will feel an enormous weight being lifted from your shoulders.

Tame the victim voice. The key to moving on is to tame the "victim voice." That bad things happen to good people is a fact of life. I'm not saying you can't feel sorry for yourself, but you don't need to give the victim voice a microphone. The victim voice will keep reminding you of how unfair everything is, how you were wronged, and how nothing is your fault. Don't listen to it. If you do, your reward will be to make the same mistakes again; that comes with the territory of nothing being your fault. Instead, accept your 10 percent, learn from the experience, and don't repeat your mistakes.

How do you know when the victim voice is calling the shots for you? Ask yourself the original question whenever you feel you were treated unfairly: *If I had a do-over, what could I have done differently?* If the answer is *nothing,* your victim voice is running the show. If the answer is literally anything else, you are on your way to not only silencing the victim voice but also accepting responsibility, learning from your mistakes, and being wiser for it. Radio personality Michael Baisden said it best: "You can never make the same mistake twice because the second time you make it, it's not a mistake, it's a choice."

Let it go. This final step is the easiest, but you've got to commit to it. Read this next sentence and consider the wisdom in its simplicity:

Let it go.

If holding on to your anger would somehow punish those responsible for your pain and make it go away, I'd tell you to hold on to it for all its worth. But it doesn't.

Let it go.

No one who really cares about you wants to keep hearing your horror stories—they want to hear about your recovery and help you move forward.

Let it go.

Each time you tell the stories, you cause yourself to relive the pain of the past. You also continue to empower those who inflicted your pain.

Let it go.

You've accepted responsibility for your part in the breakup and learned from your mistakes. You are not a victim. You don't need to rehash the past or continue reciting the stories to anyone, including yourself, ever again.

Let it go.

It's time to focus on the future and let go of the past.

Think of how extraordinary it would be to hear someone say, "It was a difficult breakup, and I was hurt and angry, but some of the responsibility was mine. I've learned from the experience, and I've moved on." That is not the voice of a victim but rather of a healthy person who has evolved and is prepared for whatever next steps life has in store.

Do not be a prisoner of the past. No matter how abused or battered you may feel, accepting some responsibility, learning from your mistakes, and letting go of your anger will set you free. And as for those who wronged you, consider the words of onetime preacher Jim Casy in *The Grapes of Wrath*: "Maybe there ain't no sin and there ain't no virtue, they's just what people does. Some things folks do is nice and some ain't so nice, and that's all any man's got a right to say."

Take responsibility, learn, let it go, and evolve. It's not about losing your faith in others; it's about regaining your faith in yourself.

Take Alliances Seriously

I am not a fan of most TV reality shows or, as I call them, "bad actors acting badly," but, oddly enough, I've always been a fan of one of the very first ones ever produced. I'm referring to the social experiment that is *Survivor*. Its lessons are many, but one of the most striking involves alliances. There are three critical aspects to aligning yourself with others: alliances are unavoidable, it is imperative to choose wisely, and loyalty is paramount.

There is no avoiding them. Many people think that when they work with others it's not necessary to form alliances. Watch *Survivor* and you'll notice how fast alliances are formed, much like they are in the workplace. I am not referring to a clique, which is an exclusive club that is often brazen in its inclusion and exclusion of others. An alliance is much subtler. By avoiding alliances, you run the risk of sending dangerous signals to others. Typically, those who duck alliances are seen as aloof and not team players. You are naive if you think that you are above alliances.

Choose wisely. This cannot be overstated. There is no rule that says you must form an alliance with the first person to reach out to you. As a matter of fact, often immediate offers to form an alliance come from those who struggle with their other alliances; thus they aggressively go after the new people. When you align with the first person to extend their hand, you are branded as someone who is in tight with them.

Season after season of *Survivor* reminds us of the importance of choosing alliances wisely. One season I remember, two of the nicest women quickly formed an alliance with a guy who reached out and appeared to be a good match, although they barely knew him. It turned out he was a loose cannon. By sheer association, those women were the first two removed from the experiment. As with most dangerously uncontrollable people, the guy managed to stay in the game far longer than he deserved. Sound familiar? As Oscar Wilde wrote in *Mr. Dumby*, "Experience is the name everyone gives to their mistakes."

Making the wrong alliances can be devastating, and choosing an alliance based solely on friendship or shared preferences is both an instinct and a mistake. It's not a question of compromising your values; it's the reality of understanding the ramifications of aligning yourself with people.

Guess what happens to good people who align with individuals who struggle within the tribe, I mean, the corporation? Predictably, they soon find themselves scrambling to convince everyone that they never really shared the views of those individuals and that they are now aligned with everyone else. Those people are often the next to be voted off the island.

Remain loyal to your alliances. The only thing worse than someone who makes poor choices is someone who flip-flops from one alliance to the next. That lack of loyalty is apparent to everyone and likely results in a reputation for being untrustworthy. Is there a worse smear professionally? Once trust is broken, it's nearly impossible to regain it. Understanding this, choosing your alliances

wisely, and remaining loyal to the choices you make
will help you succeed in the social experiment that I call
"working with others."

Learning how to sustain the belief that others have in you
does involve becoming politically astute. Understanding
the consequences of your choices and taking steps to
protect yourself is a matter of intelligently buying in to
behaviors that matter to those around you. When others
put their faith in you, like it or not, they expect you to
understand the politics of your position and behave
accordingly. When you do, you can sustain the trust that
has been placed in you.

Moving beyond Hope

It is my goal that what you've read in this book went beyond simply entertaining you, motivating you, or inspiring you. Don't get me wrong—if you got that out of this book, I'm thrilled! But I hope we can do better.

Offering solutions to issues like a lack of credibility, an inability to get others to believe you, or, worst of all, an inability to believe in yourself is a tall order to say the least. For me it all started at Xerox, but over three decades of working with audiences and individuals I desired to do more than make people feel good. Entertaining, motivating, and inspiring are terrific, but my goal was to teach. You have worked your way through a series of processes tied together with stories that formed a framework of solutions. As with any process, these ideas and techniques are useful only if you truly commit to implementing what you have learned.

Consider the crossroads that many are faced with when learning the game of golf. Do you want to marginally improve, or do you want to pour your heart and soul into succeeding? Watch amateur golfers and you'll see what I mean. You are looking at two types of golfers.

The first golfer is not very good; he has hit the ball improperly for so long that he is getting good at hitting the ball badly! There were most likely some lessons involved, and a few of the concepts taught were probably partially adhered to. There was some practice, but practice is not a lot of fun, so there probably wasn't much. There was also a nagging voice that said, *Come on, you're thinking about this so much you're actually worse now than before you took lessons! Grab a quick idea or two, learn it your way, and let's get back to getting that ball in the fairway.* There was no other voice to disagree, so what had begun as a strict way of doing things correctly became a stray idea or two done halfway. That golfer will continue to play the game at an amateur level, expecting more, changing little, and being baffled by his lack of success.

The second golfer is very good, and her success was no accident. You can tell that she took lessons, but even more importantly those concepts were strictly adhered to. There was practice—a lot of it. There was also a nagging voice; this one said, *Come on, this is just too hard. You got the ball in the fairway before you took lessons, you played a decent game, and you had fun!* But that voice was countered by another, which said, *No, I'm going to master this—and that means I need to take a step or two back before I can move forward.* That golfer went from playing a satisfactory game, to briefly playing worse, to then playing at a higher level and having more success than she ever imagined.

I wish life were as simple as the game of golf—but there's much more on the line than a great golf score. We're talking about a life score.

What will you do with the lessons you have learned?

Are you willing to challenge yourself, move out of your comfort zone, and try a new swing? Your old way of doing things is itching to convince you otherwise, so ignore that nagging voice.

You picked up this book for a reason. Another voice in your head told you to read it. Are you going to let that voice down? That voice is your authentic voice, and good for you for heeding its advice.

Now it's time to fight for your authenticity. It will require risk. It will require trial and error. It will involve success and failure. Nothing you have read in these pages will decrease your chances of success. You are challenging yourself to improve and make positive changes. I don't turn away from solutions that can only make me better.

You read this book because you have hope. I have hope, too: I hope you found some timely reminders and new ideas that will translate into your believing in yourself and helping others believe in you, too. You may have doubts, but you also now have tools and ideas in place to combat those doubts. Mastering the skills in this book requires hard work and a belief in yourself. You *are* good enough. Now go out there and make the world believe in you.

SUGGESTED
READINGS

There is no finish line for self-improvement. It's a worthy voyage, and the following books represent wonderful ideas that have the potential to assist you on your journey.

Alter, Cara Hale. *The Credibility Code: How to Project Confidence and Competence When It Matters Most.* San Francisco: Meritus Books, 2012.

Booher, Dianna. *Creating Personal Presence: Look, Talk, Think, and Act Like a Leader.* San Francisco: Berrett-Koehler, 2011.

Cuddy, Amy. *Presence: Bringing Your Boldest Self to Your Biggest Challenges.* New York: Hachette Book Group, 2015.

Donnelly, Darrin. *Think Like a Warrior: The Five Inner Beliefs that Make You Unstoppable.* Lenexa, KS: Shamrock New Media, 2016.

Goleman, Daniel. *Emotional Intelligence: Why It Can Matter More Than IQ*. New York: Bantam Books, 1995, 1997.

Hill, Napoleon. *Success through a Positive Mental Attitude*. New York: Pocket Books, 1960, 1977.

Johnson, Vic. *The Magic of Believing: Believe in Yourself and the Universe Is Forced to Believe in You*. Melrose, FL: Laurenzana Press, 2012.

King, Patrick. *Improve Your People Skills: Build and Manage Relationships, Communicate Effectively, Understand Others, and Become the Ultimate People Person*. Self-published, Amazon Digital Services, 2017. Kindle.

Kouzes, James M., and Barry Z. Posner. *Credibility: How Leaders Gain and Lose It, Why People Demand It*. San Francisco: Jossey-Bass, 2011.

Peale, Norman Vincent. *The Power of Positive Thinking*. New York: Fireside, 1952, 2003.

Tracy, Brian. *The Power of Self-Confidence: Become Unstoppable, Irresistible, and Unafraid in Every Area of Your Life*. Hoboken, NJ: John Wiley & Sons, 2012.

Tuhovsky, Ian. *The Science of Effective Communication: Improve Your Social Skills and Small Talk, Develop Charisma and Learn How to Talk to Anyone*. Self-published, CreateSpace, 2017.

ACKNOWLEDGMENTS

As with any book, there are many people to thank, but it all starts with my wife, Ronni: you don't edit just my words; you edit my life—and it's always better after you've done so.

To the remarkable Brian Tracy, your career and your teachings have been an inspiration to me. I am overjoyed that your voice is part of this book.

Bob Korzenewski and Will Yeatman, you taught me what true, selfless dedication really means. That lesson is one I will always cherish.

To my many workshop participants and mentees—my "tune-mates"— through my trials and plenty of errors you put up with some rather unorthodox attempts to crack the code of believability. Thank you for being my willing canvas to paint on.

To the amazing folks at Career Network Ministry, dedicated to helping those who struggle with unemployment, you invited me in as a speaker, allowed me to

*Just some of the incredible people who compose
the Career Network Ministry*

remain as a servant, and permitted me to humbly assist where necessary. This book reflects the journeys we took and the lessons we learned together.

To my father, Lee Jolles, you left this earth on a day, month, and year I choose to forget, but the lessons I learned from you I don't choose to just remember—I choose to implement. You taught me that when you give, you don't give with just your checkbook; you give with your time. Without that lesson I would have missed so much, including writing this book.

To my editor, Neal Maillet, you continue to give the gift of your faith in my words, and without you I'm not sure those words would have been read. You allow me to be me while skillfully reining me in from time to time when my me goes a little too far. You're not just my editor; you're my trusted friend.

To my teacher Rob Ramoy, you opened a window to acting that changed my life. Making a true, lasting impact on a student's life is the hope of any educator. Mission accomplised.

To my copyeditor, Elizabeth von Radics: It's not easy editing a manuscript with an author who is bound and determined to maintain an authentic voice. You were bound and determined to make sure that that authentic voice got it right grammatically. That takes a unique skill, which you performed beautifully, and I am grateful to have had the opportunity to work with you.

To my children—Danny, Jessie, and Sandy—I couldn't be prouder of the young man and women you have become. Someone once told me that you can be a father or you can be friend, but you can't be both. That someone was wrong. Thank you for agreeing with me because I cherish being both.

INDEX

7-38-55 rule, 71–72

90-10 principle, 154–55

Abbey, Edward, 50

acting, xvi, 82–88
   locking it down, 102–5
   method acting, 106–7

Adler Group, The, 119

ad-libs, 63–64

age concerns, 95–96

Allen, Woody, 30

alliances, 157–60

anxious, as term, 122–23

arrival time, 36–37

arrogance, fear of, 126

artists, 15–16

audience, rooting for you,
   93–95

author-clients, 101

authority, 76–78

"bad luck," xix, 111, 126

Baisden, Michael, 155

baseball examples, 76–78,
   112–15, 148–49

basketball examples, 56,
   123–24, 147–49

Beautiful Mind, A (movie), 22

belief of others (getting others
   to believe you), xix, 48–67

   develop a communication
     shot clock, 56–69

   embrace dysfunction,
     59–62

   find your communication
     rhythm, 50–52

   it is not what you know
     that makes people
     believe you, 48–50

   listening beats talking,
     65–67

   pay attention to transitions,
     62–65

   use the power of the pause,
     52–56

believing in yourself, 8–25

    allow yourself to try and fail, 13–14

    balance personal feedback, 18–20

    celebrating, 23–25

    commit to, 9–13

    control the negative voices, 21–23

    seeing yourself as others see you, 15–17

body language, 71

breakups, 153–57

Brooks, Albert, 91–93

Camelot, 34–35

Career Network Ministry (CNM), xiii–xvii

celebrating, 23–25

character, understanding, 81–88

cliques, 158

coaching yourself, 19

Collins, Jim, 150

commitment, 40–43, 99–101

communication rhythm, 50–52

communication shot clock, 56–69

condescending voice, 80–81

confidence, xvi–xvii

    accept and embrace your shortcomings, 95–98

    arrogance, fear of, 126

    don't be afraid to run in the rain, 99–101

    locking it down, 102–5

    putting a lion in your heart, 90–108

    "this" makes all the difference, 70–73

    umpire example, 76–78

    what would you attempt to do?, 105–8

    your audience is rooting for you (six words), 93–95

control, 12–13

    actions of others, 43–45

    listening beats talking, 66–67

    See also negative voices, controlling

"conversation voice," 81

courage, 29, 90. *See also* confidence

credit not given, 70–71

Damn Yankees (Abbott and Wallop), 82

Day-Lewis, Daniel, 85–86

decision-making: squirrel syndrome, 10–11

Defending Your Life (Brooks), 91–93

Desert Solitaire (Abbey), 50

details, 150–52

disagreement, managing, 142–44

disappointment, 116

disingenuous voice, 79–81

distrust, 48–49

doubt, 15, 48

dysfunction, embracing, 59–62

emotions
7-38-55 rule, 71–72
acting positively, 120–21
it's not what people hear; it's what they feel, 73–74

empathy, 55, 73

employer, managing, 134–37

An Evening with John Denver, 63

experimentation, 103–5

eye contact, 55
misreading, 137–39

facial expressions, 42, 55, 107, 144

failure
fear of, 13–14, 117
hope and, 116

fear, 107
of failure, 13–14, 117
fog of, 90–93

fear and response, 28–45
I can't control the actions of others/play the course—not the opponent, 43–45
I won't be good enough/ trust yourself, 38–40
I'm just not that interesting/commit to who you are, 40–43
I'm not as prepared as I should be/run your race, 35–38
odds are against me/ showing up, 28–32
perfection/pride in imperfection, 30–35

FedEx ad ("this"), 70, 88

feedback, balanced, xvii, 18–20

flight attendant voice, 79

focus, 114

forewarned is forearmed, 152

Gandhi, Mahatma, 142

Gangs of New York (movie), 85–86

genetics, 111

goals, 127

golf examples, 43–44, 148, 162–63

Good Morning America, 95

Good to Great (Collins), 150

Grapes of Wrath, The (Steinbeck), 157

hard skills, 4–5

Harris, Richard, 34–35

health, 110–11

hiding, 2–3

hope, 115–17
    moving beyond, 162–64

human condition, 22, 62

humility, 98

humor, 40–42

improv, xvi, 63–64

improvement, areas for, 19–20

In the Name of the Father (movie), 86

"inside voice," 79

instinct versus logic, 118–19, 127

insurance profession, 145

internal clock, 54, 57–58

interviews, 58

Jake the black lab, 97–98

jinxes (superstition), 125–27

Jolles, Lee, 56–57, 139, 150–51

knowledge
    distrust and, 48–49
    know when—and how—to be right, 139–42

Last of the Mohicans, The (movie), 86

letting go, 156

"limp," 96–98

Lincoln (movie), 85

Lincoln, Abraham, 28

listening, 53–56, 65–67

long-term goals, 102

loyalty, 157–60

luck, 112–15

lying, 49, 75

management positions, 134

marathons, 99–100

Mehrabian, Albert, 71

mental game, 44

metronome, 55

microphone-inflection voice, 79

mind-set, 44, 105–6

money, 111

more-is-better-itus, 39

movies
message, 90–92
understanding your character, 85–86

movies, rhythm of, 50–52

Mr. Dumby (Wilde), 159

My Cousin Vinny (movie), 59

My Left Foot (movie), 86

Nash, John Forbes, Jr., 22

negative voices, controlling, 21–23, 29, 40, 78, 92, 105–6, 150
victim voice, 155

nonverbal cues, 42–43, 88, 107, 144

off-hand, 148–49

office politics. *See* politics of success (office politics)

page-count goals, 101

pauses, 52–56

perfection
pride in imperfection, 30–35
repetition, 103–4

performance skills, 6

performers, 34–35, 63

personal effort, believing in yourself and, 12–13

personal style, 65

personality tests, 83–84

perspective, 123–25

Pesci, Joe, 59

politics of success (office politics), 132–60
beware of misreads, 137–39
double your efforts to address your weaknesses, 147–50
heed your own advice, 145–47

it's the little pieces that count the most, 150–52

know when—and how—to be right, 139–42

learn how to disagree, 142–44

moving past a breakup, 153–57

"playing politics," 133

principles, 133–34

step in and manage the difficult boss, 134–37

take alliances seriously, 157–60

positivity, 19, 110–30

act positively, 120–21

allow yourself to hope, 115–17

banish the word *worry*, 121–23

basic formula, 110

belief in you, not in jinxes, 125–27

keep things in perspective, 123–25

let others know what you're up to, 117–19

luck, 112–15

take stock of what you have, 128–30

practice, 114

repetition, 35, 103–4

preparation, 59, 113, 114

prepare your mind, 36–37

pressure

prepare your mind, 36–37

seeking out, 35–36

show up early, 36

visualization, 37

principles, 133–34

public announcements, 79

public image, 28

questions, 42, 53–56, 66

quitting, 28–32

Ramoy, Rob, 82–83

real voice, finding your, 79–81

rehearsing, 103–5

remembering experience, 62

repetition, 35, 103–4

responsibility, 157

risk

allow yourself to try and fail, 13–14

believing in yourself and, 10–12

Roberts, Robin, 95

role-plays, video-recording, 17–18

Roosevelt, Eleanor, 28

"running in the rain," 99–101

Schuller, Robert H., 107

seeing yourself as others see you, 15–17

self-confidence. *See* believing in yourself

self-evaluation exercise, 19–20

self-reflection, 154

Shedd, John A., 11, 13

shortcomings, accepting, 95–98

short-term commitments, 102

showing up, 28–32

showing up early, 36

silence, power of, 52–56

"singsong-presenter voice," 79–80

smartphones, 66

smiling, 121

"soft skills," 3–5

solutions, 20

Spielberg, Steven, 85

spontaneity, 34, 63–64

squirrel syndrome, 10–11

stage fright, 93

staying employed, xviii–xix

stepping up your game, 70–88
   find your real voice, 79–81
   it's not what people hear; it's what they feel, 73–74
   just tell the truth, 74–76
   say it like you mean it, 76–78
   "this" makes all the difference, 70–73
   understand your character, 81–88

"Stolen Idea" FedEx ad, 70, 88

struggle, celebration and, 23–25

stuff, distracting, 39–40

success
   politics of, 132–60
   as willingness to fail, 14

succinct message, 57–58

support/build process, 143

Survivor (reality TV show), 157–58

take stock of what you have, 128–30

team players, 141–42, 158

"teasing," 22–23

"this" makes all the difference, 70–73

timing, of disagreement, 144

Torn, Rip, 92

Tracy, Brian, 84

transitions, 62–65

   transition out, 64–65

Trump, Donald, 72–73

trust

   "knowing too much" and, 49–50

   trusting yourself, 10, 38–40

truth, telling, 74–76

trying, 13, 14, 92

   hope and, 116

   new things, 103–5

tune metaphor, xvi, 3, 72–73

   disagreement and, 143–44

   emotional impact, 73–74

Twain, Mark, 73–74

typecasting, 149–50

victim voice, 155

victory, celebrating, xv, 23–25

victory lap, xv

video-recording of self, 17–18

visualization, 37

voice, use of, 51–52

   7-38-55 rule, 71–72

   finding your real voice, 79–81

   voice drop, 64–65

voicemail test, 72

"wanting something more," 8

Washington Nationals, 112

Washington Senators, 82

weaknesses, addressing, 147–50

"What Our Internal Voices Say about Ourselves" (*Time*), 21

Wilde, Oscar, 159

wiseGEEK, 133

words, 2–3, 71, 73

   disagreement and, 143

worries, 44–45

worry, 121–23

Xerox Corporation, 17, 139–40

Zadra, Dan, 123

ABOUT THE AUTHOR

Merrill Worthington Photography

Rob Jolles is a sought-after speaker and best-selling author who teaches, entertains, and inspires audiences worldwide. For more than 30 years, he has trained, coached, and consulted with tens of thousands of individuals whose success depends on their ability to be believed. His keynotes and workshops have taken him around the world; he's accumulated more than 2.5 million miles in the air and worked with hundreds of organizations, including companies in North America, Europe, Africa, and the Far East. These programs have allowed him to connect with salespeople, managers, doctors, lawyers, parent groups, and a dozen universities and amass a client list that reads like a *Who's Who* of Fortune 500 companies, including more than 50 financial institutions.

Rob's best-selling books—including *How to Change Minds: The Art of Influence without Manipulation; Customer Centered Selling: Eight Steps to Success from the World's Best Sales Force; The Way of the Road Warrior: Lessons in Business and Life from the Road Most Traveled; How to Run Seminars & Workshops: Presentation Skills for Consultants, Trainers, Teachers, and Salespeople;* and *Mental Agility: The Path to Persuasion*—have been translated into more than a dozen languages.

As president of Jolles Associates, Inc., Rob has designed programs that teach the real-word lessons that corporations, executives, and customers desperately need to be successful. He lives in Chevy Chase, Maryland.

ABOUT JOLLES ASSOCIATES, INC.

We need to demand more from programs than just entertainment, motivation, and inspiration. That's the easy part. We must inform—and do so with true, repeatable, predictable processes to ensure lasting results.

Keynotes

Looking to put a charge into your next meeting? One- to two-hour keynote deliveries are available on a variety of topics. Presentation materials go far beyond slides and are designed to allow all who attend to capture the key elements of the delivery and truly participate.

Workshops

If you're looking not just to learn a new idea or two but to bring about true cultural change, we can accommodate. Half-day, one-day, and two-day programs are available,

incorporating small-group activities, role-plays, case studies, and Mental Agility® exercises. Presentation materials include tailored buyer briefs, case studies, simulations, participant guides, and books authored by the speaker.

For more information about programs offered by Rob Jolles and Jolles Associates, Inc:

Visit:	www.Jolles.com
Email:	Training@Jolles.com
Call:	1-703-759-7767
Write:	Jolles Associates, Inc.
	P.O. Box 30009
	Bethesda, MD 20824

Also:

Join Rob on Facebook https://www.facebook.com
/JollesAssociates/

Connect with Rob on LinkedIn https://www.linkedin
.com/in/robert-jolles-8a459b12/

Follow Rob on Twitter @robjolles

Plus:

Sign up to receive Rob's free biweekly BLArticle®:
www.jolles.com/blarticle

Part blog, part article, Rob's BLArticle is a one-of-a-kind
e-communication dedicated to inspiring, informing, and
interacting.

Also by Rob Jolles

How to Change Minds
The Art of Influence without Manipulation

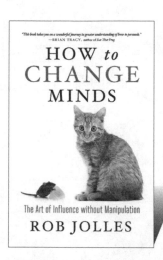

Surely you know plenty of people who need to make a change, but despite your most well-intentioned efforts, they resist because people fundamentally fear change. As a salesman, father, friend, and consultant, Rob Jolles knows this scenario all too well. Drawing on his highly successful sales background and decades of research, he lays out a simple, repeatable, predictable, and ethical process that will enable you to lead others to discover for *themselves* what and why they need to change. Whether you hope to make a sale or improve a relationship, Jolles's wise advice—illustrated through a bevy of sometimes funny, sometimes moving, always illuminating stories—will help you ensure that changing someone's mind is never an act of coercion but rather one of caring and compassion.

Paperback, 216 pages, ISBN 978-1-60994-829-0
PDF ebook, ISBN 978-1-60994-830-6
ePub ebook ISBN 978-1-60994-831-3

Berrett–Koehler Publishers, Inc.
www.bkconnection.com   **800.929.2929**

Berrett–Koehler
Publishers

Berrett-Koehler is an independent publisher dedicated to an ambitious mission: *Connecting people and ideas to create a world that works for all.*

We believe that the solutions to the world's problems will come from all of us, working at all levels: in our organizations, in our society, and in our own lives. Our BK Business books help people make their organizations more humane, democratic, diverse, and effective (we don't think there's any contradiction there). Our BK Currents books offer pathways to creating a more just, equitable, and sustainable society. Our BK Life books help people create positive change in their lives and align their personal practices with their aspirations for a better world.

All of our books are designed to bring people seeking positive change together around the ideas that empower them to see and shape the world in a new way.

And we strive to practice what we preach. At the core of our approach is Stewardship, a deep sense of responsibility to administer the company for the benefit of all of our stakeholder groups including authors, customers, employees, investors, service providers, and the communities and environment around us. Everything we do is built around this and our other key values of quality, partnership, inclusion, and sustainability.

This is why we are both a B-Corporation and a California Benefit Corporation—a certification and a for-profit legal status that require us to adhere to the highest standards for corporate, social, and environmental performance.

We are grateful to our readers, authors, and other friends of the company who consider themselves to be part of the BK Community. We hope that you, too, will join us in our mission.

A BK Business Book

We hope you enjoy this BK Business book. BK Business books pioneer new leadership and management practices and socially responsible approaches to business. They are designed to provide you with groundbreaking and practical tools to transform your work and organizations while upholding the triple bottom line of people, planet, and profits. High-five!

To find out more, visit **www.bkconnection.com**.

Berrett–Koehler
Publishers

Connecting people and ideas
to create a world that works for all

Dear Reader,

Thank you for picking up this book and joining our worldwide community of Berrett-Koehler readers. We share ideas that bring positive change into people's lives, organizations, and society.

To welcome you, we'd like to offer you a free e-book. You can pick from among twelve of our bestselling books by entering the promotional code **BKP92E** here: http://www.bkconnection.com/welcome.

When you claim your free e-book, we'll also send you a copy of our e-newsletter, the *BK Communiqué*. Although you're free to unsubscribe, there are many benefits to sticking around. In every issue of our newsletter you'll find

• A free e-book
• Tips from famous authors
• Discounts on spotlight titles
• Hilarious insider publishing news
• A chance to win a prize for answering a riddle

Best of all, our readers tell us, "Your newsletter is the only one I actually read." So claim your gift today, and please stay in touch!

Sincerely,

Charlotte Ashlock
Steward of the BK Website

Questions? Comments? Contact me at bkcommunity@bkpub.com.

Certified

Corporation
bcorporation.net